LAST NIGHT OF THE PROMS

LAST NIGHT OF THE PROMS

An Official Miscellany

Foreword by Katie Derham

BOOKS

1 3 5 7 9 10 8 6 4 2

BBC Books, an imprint of Ebury Publishing
20 Vauxhall Bridge Road,
London SW1V 2SA

BBC Books is part of the Penguin Random House group of companies whose
addresses can be found at global.penguinrandomhouse.com

Penguin
Random House
UK

Copyright © Woodland Books Ltd 2018

Text: Alison Maloney

Design: Seagull Design

Cover design: Two Associates

Illustrations: Alamy

This book is published to accompany the BBC's radio and television broadcasts
of the BBC Proms

First published by BBC Books in 2018

www.penguin.co.uk

A CIP catalogue record for this book is available from the British Library

ISBN 9781785943386

Typeset in 11/15 pt Garamond MT Std
by Integra Software Services Pvt. Ltd, Pondicherry

Printed and bound by Clays Ltd, St Ives PLC

Penguin Random House is committed to a sustainable future for our
business, our readers and our planet. This book is made from
Forest Stewardship Council® certified paper.

CONTENTS

Foreword by Katie Derham

For as long as I can remember, the BBC Proms have been part of my life. When I was growing up, my family watched the Last Night of the Proms on TV every year, and I loved it, even from a very young age. As a keen musician myself I was always fascinated by the orchestra, but I also loved watching all the balloons, the party streamers, the flags and people bobbing up and down. I could see the Prommers were all having a great time, and their enthusiasm was infectious.

Fast forward to 2010, and I was asked to present the whole season of the Proms – including the Last Night – for the BBC. It was a career-defining moment for me, a change of direction from my news background, and I couldn't possibly say no.

As well as expanding my musical horizons as a child, the Proms had been part of my awareness of British cultural life. They are right at the heart of what makes the British tick. To have the chance of being around musicians of the highest calibre – and being involved in something that is such an institution – was a dream come true.

For many people watching at home, the Last Night of the Proms may well be the one classical concert they see all year, so it is a huge honour to be there with them.

The first time I presented it, the sense of festivity and the gala element just blew me away. Even though it was a big event in our house when I was a child, I had never seen it live before I found myself presenting it, and I was really bowled over by how genuinely excited the audience was to be there. It's not easy to get a ticket to the Last Night, so being there is a big deal. There's a slight sense of Willy Wonka and the golden tickets, and a huge air of celebration.

That first 'Hello and welcome ...' was terrifying but thrilling. When the red light came on the camera I thought, 'My God! This is the Last Night of the Proms – there are millions of people watching, this is BBC One, Saturday night, it's live!'

With live TV anything can happen – and on that first occasion it did. The conductor of the BBC Symphony Orchestra was the late Jiří Bělohlávek, who was an utter sweetheart but a bit scatterbrained. He didn't play the pieces in the same order as had been decided, so we were trying to work it out as we went along. He also went offstage between pieces, unplanned, and I was hearing frantic voices in my ear saying, 'Keep talking, he's walked off. He wasn't meant to walk off. Keep talking.' I had to think on my feet – 'What can I say about the flags that we see in the audience? Can I tell more anecdotes about the Proms founder-conductor Sir Henry Wood?' It was a baptism of fire, but I loved every minute.

Because it's a live event, we always have Plan A, B, C, D, E, F and G in our back pockets. I have a lot of notes, a lot of extra information about every piece of music and about the Prommers. But in the end, as with any live event, you chuck away a lot of that because you are following the director and speaking over the camera shots. The whole thing is very fluid and I really do just go with the flow.

For me, the Proms season is a lot more than just a series of concerts of great music. It is a quintessentially British summer event. Going to a prom is more than just going to a concert. There is something about the atmosphere there, about the sense of history, about the fact that the audience is made up of people from all walks of life. And the venue, of course, is spectacular. Going to the Royal Albert Hall for any kind of event is a special treat, but for the Proms it has a particular resonance. You know you are witnessing the best musicians in the world and yet it's not exclusive, and always feels welcoming and friendly.

As well as the music, the Prommers – the audience members who've queued up for a standing space in the arena or gallery – really make for a unique experience. Some are a little eccentric, it's true. But they are all genuine music lovers. Many of them have been coming to the Proms for decades; some come to every single concert. They're charming, enthusiastic, and I love the quirky traditions of their chants and the calls, for instance when the piano is moved onto the stage. They raise many thousands of pounds for charity every year, too.

The Proms season for me is a wonderful, hectic time and I love every concert, but the Last Night holds a special place in my heart. I love the *Fantasia on British Sea-Songs* and the way it changes slightly every year. I look forward to the speech by the conductor and I am always moved by 'Land of Hope and Glory'. As the chords strike up for that, you can feel the whole audience gearing up. It's like a collective intake of breath before everyone starts singing, and it's magical.

There is something about that gala feeling that is very engaging. It enthuses you and fills you with excitement, and, after eight weeks of concerts, there's a demob-happy feeling backstage as well.

For the country as a whole it's slightly bittersweet. The Last Night of the Proms signals the end of the summer, it's back to school and autumn is here. But why not go out with a bang? For me, the Last Night is a real celebration of everything that is good about music, about people and about having fun. And what a swell party it is!

CHAPTER I

HOW
IT ALL
BEGAN

'The Proms have become a symbol for accessible, highest-quality music-making around the whole world'

– Sakari Oramo, Chief Conductor, BBC Symphony Orchestra

When it comes to the Proms – and the famous Last Night – one man in particular has become indelibly associated with its beginnings. Sir Henry Wood, whose bronze bust adorned with a laurel chaplet looks out across the audience throughout each season, is a familiar name to seasoned Promenaders as the conductor who brought the classics to the masses.

But there are other individuals too, less well known to the general public, who deserve wider acclaim. One in particular is Robert Newman. After all, it was he who had the idea for the Proms in the first place.

AN IDEA AND A MISSION

'I am going to run nightly concerts and train the public by easy stages – popular at first, gradually raising the standard until I have created a public for classical and modern music.' So said Robert Newman to Henry Wood in 1894. These prophetic words were to lead to what has become the world's greatest classical music festival.

In the eighteenth century, outdoor promenades were a popular entertainment among the professional classes who strolled in the public gardens of London, where familiar tunes of the day would be played from a bandstand. Classical music was for the rich and privileged who could afford the expensive ticket prices to indoor concerts. The poorest in the community rarely had access to music of any kind, but those with a little money to spare enjoyed popular – and sometimes bawdy – songs in music halls. Here, acts performed whilst the audience ate, drank, chatted or joined in with the singing. Cultured it was not, but there was a great sense of merriment and enjoyment.

Robert Newman, however, had a plan to bring classical music to all classes ... at affordable prices. Born into a wealthy family in 1858, he studied singing in Italy and then worked at the London Stock Exchange, singing bass in his spare time. He began organising orchestral concerts and became the first lessee and manager of the newly built concert venue the Queen's Hall in Langham Place, London. A natural entrepreneur, Newman set about putting his vision into practice and found financial backing from throat specialist Dr George Cathcart.

Newman decided against a star conductor and instead in 1895 offered the little-known 26-year-old Henry Wood the opportunity to be sole conductor throughout an eight-week musical festival called 'Mr Robert Newman's Promenade Concerts'.

Whereas a typical ticket for a normal symphony concert would cost anything between five shillings (25p – or equivalent to £27 today) and one pound (£108 today) for the best seats, Newman introduced a season ticket for the duration of his Promenade Concerts costing just a guinea (£1.05), the equivalent of £113 today. Seats were removed to provide a standing area for Prommers paying a shilling (about £5.40 today) for one night. Here, he fostered an informal atmosphere by copying the practice of music halls and encouraging people to eat, drink and smoke – the only stipulation being that gentlemen must not strike matches whilst the orchestra was playing!

Wood, who had attended the Royal Academy of Music and now worked as a vocal coach and occasional conductor at small venues around the country, was delighted to be given such an elevated role and threw himself into it with enthusiasm.

HENRY WOOD

Henry Wood was born into a musical family in Oxford Street, London. His father, Joseph, a jeweller and engineering modeller, was an amateur cellist and sang as principal tenor in the choir of St Sepulchre-without-Newgate, in London. Wood's mother, Martha, played the piano and sang.

The couple encouraged their only child with his musical interests. His mother gave him piano lessons, and he also learned to play the violin and viola. It was at St Sepulchre that he became fascinated by the sight and sound of the organ, and the resident organist, George Cooper, invited him into the organ loft, where he gave him his first lesson.

Wood entered the Royal Academy of Music at the age of 17, studying harmony and composition, organ and piano. His ambition was to become a singing teacher, and after leaving the Academy he built a very successful practice providing private lessons. He also worked as a musical accompanist and branched out into conducting at various venues around the country.

After the conductor Felix Mottl employed him as his assistant and chorus master for a series of Wagner concerts at the newly built Queen's Hall, Wood was spotted by Robert Newman, who invited him to conduct the season of promenades he was planning. It was here that he flourished and established a name for himself, building a familiar pattern and repertoire for the Proms over the years, including his much-loved *Fantasia on British Sea-Songs*. His attention to detail, flair and promotion of up-and-coming musical talents were much admired.

In 1898 he married one of his singing pupils, Olga Michailoff, and would often accompany her on the piano at her singing recitals. After a short illness Olga died in 1909 and two years later Wood married his secretary, Muriel Ellen Greatrex, with whom he had two daughters. In the same year he was knighted.

Wood was offered the conductorship of the New York Philharmonic Orchestra but he declined as he felt it was his duty to devote himself to the British public.

By the early 1930s Wood had become estranged from both his wife and his daughters, with Muriel taking the lion's share of his money and moving abroad. In 1934 he began a long-term relationship with a former pupil, Jessie Linton, who was widowed. One member of the orchestra later claimed that the new romance halted Sir Henry's decline and put him back on track. The violist Bernard Shore observed, 'She changed him. He had been badly dressed, awful clothes. Jessie got him a new evening suit, instead of the mouldy green one, and he flourished yellow gloves and a cigar ... he became human.'

Muriel, however, refused to divorce him, so his new love changed her name by deed poll to Lady Jessie Wood and was assumed by the public to be Wood's wife.

Sir Henry died on 19 August 1944, aged 75. After his death, the concerts were officially renamed the 'Henry Wood Promenade Concerts'.

'I feel I must take the credit for bringing orchestral music to the people at the price that the people could afford. Night after night this packed audience listened to all schools of orchestral music and I must say that it is the loveliest audience to make music to in the world'

– Henry Wood

QUITE ENGLISH?

Henry Wood had quite an exotic appearance as a young man. The flowing locks and beard and waxed moustache were not at all like most leading British musicians, composers, conductors of that period. In 1898, when Queen Victoria summoned Henry Wood and the Queen's Hall Orchestra to perform at Windsor Castle, she said to him, 'Mr Wood, are you quite English?'

ROBERT NEWMAN

Newman worked in the London Stock Exchange before his love of singing took him to Italy to study. On his return to England he became a concert agent and gained valuable experience organising concerts with Frederic Hyman Cowen at Covent Garden.

In 1893 he became the first manager of the Queen's Hall and hired Henry Wood as the conductor of a series of 'promenade concerts'.

Successful as the Proms continued to be in the coming years, they never created much of an income to cover costs. Newman, who had the blood of an impresario coursing through him, ran into financial difficulties in his other non-musical business interests and was unable to pay the orchestra after 1901. Fortunately, the reputation of the concerts was by then so well established that the banker Edgar Speyer took over the expense of funding them.

Newman received a knighthood in 1911. He died in 1926 and a memorial was placed in the Queen's Hall – a small plate behind his usual seat in the second circle.

THE QUEEN'S HALL

This impressive building in Langham Place, near London's Regent Street, opened in 1893. A beautiful art nouveau rotunda, the magnificent façade, made of Portland stone, featured the busts of famous composers including Beethoven, Mozart, Haydn and Bach.

It had two halls. The small one was used for recitals, small band performances and the showing of early motion pictures. The larger one, seating 2,500, was to become home to the Proms.

Audiences were delighted by the fountain in the middle, with goldfish, waterlilies and pebbles. The upholstery was Venetian red, and large, red-fringed lampshades hung low over the orchestra. The grey and terracotta paintwork around the stalls was hung with mirrors, providing sparkle and the illusion of extra space, whilst elaborately painted cupids on the ceiling looked down from on high. A peculiarity was that the main arena where the orchestra played was below ground. When you walked in you were on the level of the dress circle and would need to go downstairs to occupy the stalls. Here the seats were cheaper and if you arrived early enough, as soon as the doors opened, it was possible to nab an unreserved ticket for two shillings.

THE SOUND OF MUSIC

The Queen's Hall had superb acoustics. The narrowness of the arena – just over 26 metres – not only gave a feeling of intimacy but aided sound quality. It was helped by the wood panelling that lined the walls, creating a cavity behind 'like a violin', according to one eminent architect. Another key element was that the horseshoe-shaped seating area in front of the raised orchestra was all on the same level. Tiered seats, said baritone Roy Henderson, 'simply kill an acoustic. You're singing straight into people.' The Queen's Hall became London's premier concert venue.

'Queen's Hall means to me a great part of my musical education. In those days the education of a boy violinist, a so-called prodigy, was narrow. Henry Wood concerts were really a classroom for me'

– Joseph Szigeti, violinist

THE FIRST ORCHESTRA

Wood set about building an orchestra for the inaugural season to play at all of the 49 concerts. The Queen's Hall Orchestra comprised 80 players. Later, in 1915, its name was changed to the New Queen's Hall Orchestra, and for 32 years it appeared in every Proms season at the Queen's Hall under Henry Wood's direction.

PITCH PERFECT

Pitch and tuning were crucially important. In the first season Newman's financial backer, Dr George Cathcart, had two conditions before he would sign the cheque. The first was that Henry Wood conducted every concert, and the second, more obscure demand was that the orchestra play at a lower pitch, already adopted in Europe, which was a semitone below the English standard. Why? Because Dr Cathcart was an ear, nose and throat specialist and believed the English pitch was damaging to singers' voices.

As the musicians were loath to fork out on new low-pitched instruments, Dr Cathcart imported a whole set from Europe and lent them to the orchestra, who eventually grew to love them and bought them from him. And with typical ingenuity and resourcefulness, Henry Wood had a tuning designed, which is now preserved at the Royal Academy of Music. It was intended to make sure that the players all kept to the new 'A'.

THE FIRST NIGHT OF THE FIRST PROMS

An audience of 2,500 filled the Queen's Hall on Saturday 10 August 1895. At 8pm, Henry Wood emerged from the heavy curtains and strode along the platform to lead the orchestra in the national anthem.

Once the audience had settled, the sound of Wagner's *Rienzi* overture filled the hall. Pieces by the likes of Haydn, Liszt, Chopin and Bizet were also played. The programme, like those to come, lasted around three hours. The first half, prior to the interval, tended to have the more 'serious' music, whilst the second half was a little more populist.

As this first season went on, a pattern developed whereby Monday nights were devoted to Wagner, Fridays to Beethoven and Saturdays were reserved for more popular music. It was noted that the more relaxed second half was hugely enjoyed by the audience, in particular by those standing in front of the orchestra, unused to classical music, who had paid for the cheaper tickets.

The first Proms season was a success, and was well received by the public and critics. However, Cathcart later revealed that all but two of the concerts had made a loss of 'not less than £50' each – around £5,300 in today's money. The only profitable concerts were those where the singer Sims Reeves performed, and they were a sell-out.

'A conductor must have a complete general knowledge of music. He must have more than a slight acquaintance with every instrument in the orchestra.
He must play the piano well. He must have an impeccably sensitive ear as well as rhythmic and interpretive sense. He must be unafraid of the art of gesture. He must be a perfect sight reader and sound musician. He must study the art of singing.

He must have a good physique, a good
temper and a strong sense of discipline.
The conductor's life should be one of
self-discipline first and last'

— Henry Wood, from his book *About Conducting*

THE FIRST LAST NIGHT

The official first Last Night took place on 5 October 1895. The programme included Sir Arthur Sullivan's 'The Sailor's Grave', Leslie Stuart's 'The Bandolero' and Stanley Hawley's 'The Bells'. It finished with Hermann Louis Koenig's rousing *Post Horn Galop*, followed by the national anthem.

TAKING SHAPE

The Last Night, as we now know it, really began to take shape after Henry Wood composed *Fantasia on British Sea-Songs*. Celebrating the centenary of the Battle of Trafalgar, it was first performed not on the Last Night but at a concert on Saturday 21 October 1905. It was a night to remember. The audience loved the mix of storytelling sea shanties and big, bold patriotic blockbusters such as Handel's 'See, the Conqu'ring Hero Comes' and Arne's 'Rule, Britannia!'.

The concert ended with Elgar's *Pomp and Circumstance March No. 1 in D major*, otherwise known as 'Land of Hope and Glory'. This was first performed at the Proms on 22 October 1901 – the closing tune before the interval. At that time there were no lyrics, but the tune received a mighty applause and demands for an encore, not once but twice!

'The people simply rose and yelled,' Wood later recalled. 'I had to play it again – with the same result. It was the one and only time in the history of the Promenade concerts that an orchestral item accorded a double encore.'

By 1908, 'Fantasia' was firmly established as a Last Night regular. But it was to be a while before 'Land of Hope and Glory' was a staple part of the finale proceedings.

ALL AT SEA

In Henry Wood's autobiography *My Life of Music* (1938), he wrote about creating *Fantasia on British Sea-Songs*:

'I thought of everything that could be said to be remotely connected with the sea or to reflect British seamanship. I put down a programme beginning with Mackenzie's *Britannia Overture* and followed it with "The Bay of Biscay", "Hearts of Oak", Tchaikovsky's *1812 Overture*, "The Death of Nelson" [a hugely popular song from the opera *The Americans* (1811)]. This seemed to be all I could think of, but we [Robert Newman] felt we ought to have a real popular climax to a programme of this kind. Three weeks before the concert I conceived the idea of orchestrating and arranging a fantasia on British Sea-Songs – I collected everything I could find and put down the titles. I visited Besson's, Boosey's, Potter's, Hawkes and Rudal Carte's in order to obtain the correct naval "calls" and to find their proper order. Through the kindness of various members of these firms, I was able to do this and to make my fanfares authentic. I then set to work on my score and in due course the fantasia was put into rehearsal ... Lewis Waller recited Kipling's "Ballad of the Camperdown" and the singers were Lloyd Chandos and Robert Radford. I never dreamed when I arranged this item – merely to finish a programme for a special occasion – that the Promenade public would demand its repetition on the last night of the season for ever afterwards.'

'Jack's the Lad (Hornpipe)' was always a 'Fantasia' favourite. The real start of the frenzy to come! Wood said of it,

'They stamp their feet in time to the hornpipe – that is until I whip up the orchestra accelerando which leaves behind all those whose stamping technique is not of the very finest quality. I like to win by two bars, if possible; but sometimes have to be content with a bar and a half. It is good fun and I enjoy it as much as they.'

FIRST WORLD WAR

After the outbreak of war in 1914, Newman, Wood and Speyer discussed the future of concerts at the Queen's Hall and decided that the Proms should continue. However, anti-German feeling compelled Edgar Speyer who, although born in New York, had German Jewish parents, to return to America.

There was a campaign to ban all German music from concerts but Newman released a statement declaring that German music would be played as normal, poetically stating, 'The greatest examples of Music and Art are world possessions and unassailable even by the prejudices and passions of the hour.'

After Speyer left Britain in 1915, sheet music publishing company Chappell & Co. took over financial responsibility for the Proms and the resident orchestra had a name change to the New Queen's Hall Orchestra.

Concerts continued throughout the war years, but there were some scary moments. The hall was damaged by a falling bomb during one concert. A member of Wood's choir recalled,

'There was a crash, and then a cracking sound, and a shower of plaster began to fall from the roof of the promenade, which was packed. There was a bit of a rush from the centre of the hall for a moment. One or two of the orchestra disappeared from their seats. Even Sir Henry Wood himself glanced rather anxiously up at the roof, though still wielding his baton. After the concert no one was allowed to leave the hall. One of the orchestra nobly returned to the platform and struck up a waltz. We were soon dancing over the floor and really enjoying the experience. We were not released till about 1am.'

'When it comes to the singing of "Rule, Britannia!" we reach a climax that only Britons can reach, and I realise I can be nowhere in the world but in my native England'

– Henry Wood

GIVING IT SOME STICK

Broadcaster and long-time Proms presenter Richard Baker recalled making his first visit to the Queen's Hall for the Last Night in 1936, when he was 11:

'It was enormously exciting. The behaviour of the Promenaders was more genteel in those days. There wasn't the same degree of shouting as now. During the famous hornpipe in Henry Wood's *Fantasia on British Sea-Songs* people tapped with their umbrellas and sticks, rather than stamping. As the applause went on at the end of the concert, I remember Wood walked off and on several times and then finally he came on with his overcoat over his shoulder and his walking stick in his hand and he waved his hat at the audience and wandered off and that was the end. I must say, it was an enormously exciting thing for a lad of 11.'

BORN LEADER

Conducting a different programme every night, Wood needed to be in command of a large repertoire. Just as important, his Queen's Hall Orchestra had to be organised with meticulous efficiency. He marked his scores with copious instructions to show exactly how he wanted a piece played – which he needed to do because he had very little rehearsal time. At the beginning, he had only three rehearsals of three hours each for the whole of the six proms per week.

'He had the most colossal strength to do that. Some did say he butchered his way through things, which is a bit cruel, but that gives you the idea of the endurance and determination. Sir Henry was a very business-like man. He ran his orchestra perfectly. We would never dare be a minute late. It was all worked out in his brain what he was going to do with those three hours'

— Sidonie Goossens, harpist, Queen's Hall Orchestra

'No other conductor that I know could have done it. They would have been all at sea. He was the only one that really organised everything absolutely to the last moment.'

— Roy Henderson, baritone, who performed under Wood at the Queen's Hall

A DOG'S LIFE

Henry Wood was fond of his dog, a Scottish terrier called Michael. In his book *My Life of Music*, he writes:

'In March 1936, Rachmaninoff had lunch with us in our home in Elsworthy Road. There were other guests and, of course, our Scottie, Michael. Michael always had his chair at the table – not to be fed, but to take his place with the company. He sat upright, supporting himself with his front paws on the edge of the table, looking on. He had an "I'm one of the party" interest in all the proceedings. His head would move in the direction of each speaker.

'For a long time Rachmaninoff did not appear to notice the dog. Then he suddenly exclaimed: "Where did you get your Michael? He is human. I have bought a Scottie for my daughter, but I have never seen anything so intelligent as your Michael."

'Alas! When Rachmaninoff came to see us again in March 1938 he was horrified to see a change in our friend. "Michael is going to die," he told us, and die our little dog did on 22 April. Eleven years of sweet friendship were over.'

WOOD WAS THE FIRST CONDUCTOR TO . . .

♪ Set the standard procedure of grouping his violins together on the stage rather than separating them.
♪ Suppress audience applause between movements of a symphony.
♪ Share his applause with the orchestra.
♪ Demand that players attend all rehearsals.
♪ Admit women to his orchestra.

A SINGER'S LIFE

Despite his fame as a conductor, Wood found time all through his life to give singing lessons. He wrote a work called *The Gentle Art of Singing*, but his advice was anything but gentle. Rather it was a daunting and methodically planned daily routine of exercises drawn up with Wood's customary precision, as this extract shows …

Before Breakfast: Half an hour's physical exercise.

8.30–9: Walk in all weathers.

9: Paperwork. Transposing your songs, arias and exercises. Writing out the words of all your songs and arias. Making your own literal translations of all foreign songs and arias.

10: Breathing exercises.

10.10: Vocal exercises.

10.20: Rest voice. Work mentally at your vocal exercises.

10.30: Do not hum or sing.

10.50: Vocal exercises.

1: Rest.

11: Practise the pianoforte.

12: Ear training exercises. Interval training exercise.

1: Rest. Walk for one hour.

3: Memorise notes and words of tomorrow's work. Study languages, phrenology, phonetics and read all the standard poetical works.

4: Vocal exercises.

4.15: Read and study musical history.

5: Rest.

6: Practise the pianoforte and look over the words and music of any work you might be going to hear this week.

On three nights a week, if possible, attend a performance of an opera, an oratorio, a chamber music concert or a vocal recital.

Be in bed every night at ten o'clock, when not out at a concert.

Wood was critical of home-grown singers, as he pointed out in a 1938 interview with the *Observer* newspaper …

'The technique of the modern musician has gone up by leaps and bounds; it is staggering. I wish one could be equally enthusiastic about our singers. Many think that because they have been given the gift of a good voice, it is enough, and, alas, we miss the great singing teachers of the past. Although we have a few jolly good singers, vocal technique in this country is at a very low ebb.

'I adore singing. A fresh voice, a fresh personality, with the ear as umpire; there is nothing better. It took me thirty years to write *The Gentle Art of Singing*, and the subject, even then, was not exhausted. With many of our people there is distortion, artificiality, "mouthing", if you like. But they do not sing properly. The tone does not flow.

'So many make the mistake of singing from the diaphragm instead of from the chest. None of the really great singers make that mistake.'

BACH-ING UP THE WRONG TREE

In 1929 an orchestral arrangement of Bach's Toccata and Fugue in D minor was introduced at the Proms.

It was attributed to Paul Klenovsky. Only years later was it revealed that this was the pseudonym used by Henry Wood.

Wood explained that he had come up with the subterfuge to play a practical joke on his critics. 'I got very fed up with them, always finding fault with any arrangement or orchestrations that I made,' he said later. He added that the press 'fell into the trap and said the scoring was wonderful, Klenovsky had the real flare [sic] for true colour etc. – and performance after performance was given and asked for.'

When he finally revealed his joke, five years on, the press entered into the spirit of it and The Times ran a jocular tribute to the lamented Klenovsky.

SARGENT GIVES ORDER

After Wood's death, Adrian Boult, Basil Cameron and Constant Lambert shared conducting duties at the Proms before the baton was passed on to Malcolm Sargent in 1948. It was the flamboyant Sargent, in his element on the Last Night, who was to set the pattern for today's familiar rousing closing sequence.

It took Sargant a while to find the winning formula. After conducting the first half of the Last Night in 1948, he handed over the baton to Basil Cameron to manage the second half, which included 'Fantasia'. The following year he preceded it with 'Land of Hope and Glory'. From

1950 to 1952 the pattern was 'Land of Hope and Glory' and 'Fantasia'.

In May 1951 Sargent and Boult directed a dedication concert for the newly built Royal Festival Hall in the presence of King George VI, Princess Elizabeth, the prime minister, the Archbishop of Canterbury and much of the British establishment. The highlight of the evening was when Sargent conducted 'Land of Hope and Glory' followed by Hubert Parry's spine-tingling 'Jerusalem'. The audience stood and cheered, and the king later told Sargent that he had never been so moved by any music.

In 1953, the year that saw the coronation of Queen Elizabeth II, Sargent alone conducted the Last Night of the Proms at the Royal Albert Hall and added the rapturously received 'Jerusalem' as well as 'Rule, Britannia!' to the mix, but he dropped 'Fantasia'.

But by 1954 he had struck on the perfect formula: Elgar's *Pomp and Circumstance No. 1* with 'Land of Hope and Glory', Wood's *Fantasia on British Sea-Songs,* Arne's 'Rule, Britannia!' and Parry's 'Jerusalem'. After the playing of the national anthem would came the conductor's speech. Finally, he had it.

'They said there wasn't a public for great music 47 years ago. The critics wagged their heads. But Robert Newman said we would make a public, and we did'

– Henry Wood

CHAPTER 2

THE BBC SAVES THE PROMS

'Britain and the adjacent parts of Europe are to become one great Queen's Hall. Sir Henry Wood's sceptre is to be waved not before a thousand subjects but before hundreds of thousands – perhaps millions'

– Percy Scholes, music critic

In the mid-1920s, Henry Wood suffered a double set-back that put the future of the Proms in serious jeopardy. Cue the BBC …

WITHDRAWING FINANCE

Robert Newman's death after a brief illness in November 1926 shook Wood to the core. 'I feared everything would come to a standstill for I had never so much as engaged an extra player without having discussed it with him first,' he later recalled.

Newman's assistant, W.W. Thompson, took over as manager of the orchestra and the concerts, but the Proms suffered a second blow when, even at this difficult time, Chappell & Co. withdrew financial support. William Boosey, managing director of Chappells, objected to the 1927 Proms being broadcast by the newly formed British Broadcasting Corporation, fearing that it would damage the future of live concerts. He was not alone in the entertainment industry in regarding the BBC as a serious competitor. Theatres, concert promoters and record companies were up in arms about the new national radio network, and some agents refused to let their comedians and entertainers sign up for broadcasts because it was thought it would damage their music hall credentials and make their material 'stale'. Even Newman, before his untimely death, had attempted to prevent anyone who wished to perform at the Queen's Hall from broadcasting for the BBC.

A NEW ERA

The BBC took over from Chappell & Co. in 1927 as the new sponsor of the Proms. Having faced the prospect of the Proms coming to an end, Wood was greatly relieved and quickly appreciated the newfound freedom the change brought about.

Chappells had always heavily promoted its own music at the Proms. Not only did it sell sheet music there, but the second half of the concerts featured many of Chappells' songs. Now they were gone, it meant that Sir Henry Wood had a free rein and could choose music entirely on merit.

On the first night under the BBC's control, the music after the interval included pieces by Schubert, Handel, Rossini, Liszt, Quilter and Parry. Wood was delighted to find that the BBC gave him twice the amount of rehearsal time he had previously enjoyed, and he was also allowed extra musicians when large scores called for them instead of having to re-score the works to fit.

A reviewer in *The Times* newspaper described the changes in August 1927:

> 'The only scope for real improvement was in the second part of the programme, and the opportunity offered has been seized. We need no longer … seek refuge in the vestibule from "platitunes" about June and little cottages, but can stay to enjoy songs by Schubert or Strauss or Parry.'

The BBC saw that in broadcasting the Proms they were fulfilling General Manager John Reith's pledge to 'inform, educate and entertain'. And this too was perfectly in tune with Wood's mission from the start. Now the Proms would be reaching a far wider audience than ever before. No longer was the music contained in London – now it could be heard across the country.

THE FIRST RADIO BROADCAST

In the opening week of the 32nd season of the Proms in 1927, the BBC broadcast the first prom and two others, then roughly one a week throughout the season. The opening concert began with the national anthem followed by Elgar's *Cockaigne (In London Town)*.

This is how the programme was listed in the *Radio Times*:

The 'Proms', which since 1895 have been the most popular series of concerts in London, were, for various reasons, to have come to an end last year. However, by arrangement with the B.B.C., it has been found possible to continue the series. The Thirty-Second Season opens tonight at the Queen's Hall under the baton of Sir Henry Wood, whose name has been associated with the concerts since their initiation. During the season, which ends on September 24, the 'Proms' will frequently be broadcast from all stations.

THE PROGRAMME

Relayed from the Queen's Hall
Sir Henry J. Wood and his Symphony Orchestra

8.0
God Save the King

Overture, 'Cockaigne', Elgar
Minuet in A for Strings, Boccherini

Rosina Buckman
Aria, 'Elizabeth's Greeting' (Tannhäuser), Wagner
Arthur De Greef
Pianoforte Concert in A Minor, Grieg

Dale Smith
Three Sea-Songs: Drake's Drum; Devon, O Devon;
    The Old 'Superb', Stanford

The Orchestra
Valse Triste, Sibelius
Largo in G, Handel
Overture to William Tell, Rossini

9.40
Interlude from the Studio

9.55 app
Part II

The Orchestra
Hungarian Rhapsody No. 2, Lizst

Rosina Buckman
Who is Sylvia? Schubert
Music When Soft Voices Die, Quilter
A Birthday, Parry

Dale Smith
How Can Ye Gang, Lassie; Leezie Lindsay, Old Scotch
aire, arr. Malcolm Lawson
Mowing the Barley, Old English, arr. Cecil Sharp

The Orchestra
Prelude and Mazurka, Delibes

Contributors
Conductor: Sir Henry J. Wood
Soprano: Rosina Buckman
Baritone: Dale Smith
Pianoforte: Arthur De Greef

THE MAKING OF THE BBC SYMPHONY ORCHESTRA

♪ Almost from the beginning of its formation on 18 October 1922, the British Broadcasting Company (BBC) had broadcast from its '2LO' transmitter its own musical ensembles, such as the 2LO Light Orchestra.

♪ After the BBC started to broadcast performances by the British National Opera Company from the Royal Opera House, John Reith invited the opera company's musical director, Percy Pitt, to be the BBC's part-time musical adviser from May 1923.

♪ The BBC's first symphony concert was conducted by Pitt in 1923.

♪ In 1925 Pitt, now working full-time for the BBC as Director of Music, expanded the regular eight-piece ensemble to form the BBC Wireless Orchestra of 18 players, augmented to 37 for important broadcasts.

♪ The BBC Symphony Orchestra (BBC SO) was formed in 1930 by the BBC's new Director of Music, Adrian Boult, and became the principal orchestra for the Proms.

♪ Lord Reith wanted the new orchestra to rival the much-lauded Berlin Philharmonic, so the new formation was 114 musicians who could split into four segments for smaller concerts.

♪ It gave its first concert on 22 October 1930, conducted by Boult at the Queen's Hall.

ORCHESTRA AT WAR

After the BBC temporarily withdrew as Proms sponsors at the outbreak of war in 1939, the BBC SO moved to Bristol in order to minimise disruption to music broadcasts. But many of the musicians were also young men, and that meant call-up papers. More than 40 were released for active service in total, including 30 of the youngest, and the orchestra shrunk to 70, increasing to 90 as the war rumbled on.

During 1940 and 1941 Bristol suffered devastation from German air raids, which heavily targeted the docks, and evening concerts were among the casualties. The BBC SO began to record their music in the afternoons, to be broadcast by engineers in the evening, so that players and audiences didn't need to venture out at night.

In September 1941 the orchestra moved to the safer haven of Bedford, where it remained, giving live broadcasts and making recordings. Broadcasts were recorded at the Corn Exchange in Bedford, but because this was still a functioning corn exchange there were times when an alternative venue was needed, and so Studio 7 was created in the Great Hall at Bedford School. With its wooden galleries it had excellent acoustics.

At the end of the war, in 1945, the BBC SO returned permanently to its London base at the BBC's Maida Vale Studios, where it remains today. From there it makes regular recordings for Radio 3, many of which are free for the public to attend.

CHIEF CONDUCTORS OF THE BBC SYMPHONY ORCHESTRA

1. Adrian Boult   1930–1950
2. Malcolm Sargent   1950–1957
3. Rudolf Schwarz   1957–1962
4. Antal Doráti   1962–1966
5. Colin Davis   1967–1971
6. Pierre Boulez   1971–1975
7. Rudolf Kempe   1976
8. Gennady Rozhdestvensky   1978–1981
9. John Pritchard   1982–1989
10. Andrew Davis   1989–2000
11. Leonard Slatkin   2000–2004
12. Jiří Bělohlávek   2006–2012
13. Sakari Oramo   2013–present

PROMENADING TO THE TOP

David Pickard was a regular Promenader in his youth. He went on to become, among many things, General Director of Glyndebourne before being appointed to his current exalted position as Director of the BBC Proms in 2016. He credits the Proms for his life in music ...

'I Prommed myself a lot when I was younger. Like many people, my very first experience of live classical music was standing in the arena at the Proms. I think I was about 16 and I probably wouldn't have had a career in music had I not had that first experience.

'You will find that many people today who are either working in the arts or are performers themselves, had their first experience at the Proms. It's an incredibly important way of introducing people to classical music. One of the great things about Promming is that you are standing in the best place in the Hall and, not only that, you have paid less for it then you would for a sandwich down the road in South Kensington. It is an extraordinary bargain.'

THE BBC SYMPHONY CHORUS

♪ In 1928 the BBC decided it needed to develop a large amateur chorus of its own and this led to the formation of the National Chorus, who gave their first performance later that year in Granville Bantock's oratorio *The Pilgrim's Progress*.

♪ Early performances included UK premieres of Bartók's *Cantata Profana*, Stravinsky's *Perséphone* and Mahler's Eighth Symphony. This commitment to new music continues today.

♪ The choir's name was changed to the BBC Chorus in 1932 and again in 1935 to become the BBC Choral Society.

♪ In 1977 it became the BBC Symphony Chorus, making its first appearance under that name performing *A Sea Symphony* by Ralph Vaughan Williams on 12 October 1977.

♪ As resident chorus at the Proms, the BBC Symphony

Chorus usually performs both on the First and Last Night.

♪ Sir Andrew Davis, Chief Conductor of the BBC Symphony Orchestra from 1989 to 2000, is president of the Chorus.

♪ Neil Ferris was appointed as Chorus Director from May 2017.

CHORUS MASTERS THROUGH THE DECADES:

1. Stanford Robinson	1928–1932	
2. Cyril Dalmaine	1932–1933	
3. Leslie Woodgate	1934–1961	
4. Peter Gellhorn	1961–1972	
5. John Poole	1968–1976 (although Poole took responsibility, Gellhorn remained as official chorus director until 1972)	
6. Brian Wright	1976–1984	
7. Gareth Morrell	1984–1988	
8. Stephen Jackson	1989–2015	
9. Neil Ferris	2017–present	

THE ART OF MANAGEMENT

Paul Hughes, General Manager of the BBC Symphony Orchestra and Chorus, and the BBC Singers is a veteran of 20 BBC Proms. He is instrumental in planning and arranging and knows the pressures and pleasures of being an integral part of the BBC Proms.

What does your work with the Proms entail?

'My job, by and large, is working with the director of the Proms to make sure that the programme that we've got and the programmes that he wants line up; that we are working together to get the conductors we want for each season and decide what the key works will be.

'In our discussions we will want to make sure that the season balances and that it does not exhaust the orchestra. Doing twelve different programmes in two months is an enormous responsibility and it's tough, particularly when you've got great big works running through the season. But if there ever was any hint that they might do fewer concerts in order to give them an easier time, I think the orchestra wouldn't be happy. They love the Proms and they really look forward to it. They love the fact that the Hall is full for the concerts. It's exciting. And they get to do lots of core repertoire and interesting new works. So it's a really big deal for everybody, and my job is to co-ordinate it and make sure that the orchestra is really delivering the goods, and then getting out of the way while my management team and stage and concert management teams step in and do what they know how to do best.'

What is the breakdown of the BBC SO in terms of the various instruments?

'When we have a full orchestra we have about 98 musicians on contract, although not all are full-time.

'In strings we have 16 first violins, 14 second violins, 12 violas, 10 cellos and eight double basses. We have two harps, four percussion, including timpani, four of each woodwind

– which includes things like bass clarinet and contrabassoon
– then there are six horns, three trombones, a tuba and four
trumpets.'

What is the maximum number of players you would have on the Last Night of the Proms?

'It depends on the repertoire. If we are playing *The Planets*,
for example, it would require an orchestra of 114. So we
will bring in some freelancers for that and they will be
people we have auditioned and know.'

Do the contracted musicians bring their own instruments to the Proms or are they owned by the BBC?

'Mostly they own their own instruments. The only ones we
own are some percussion and the timpani. But most of the
time all the instruments are looked after, insured and transported for the musicians by the BBC. Carting a double bass
around on public transport is not an easy thing, and harps
are notoriously heavy and cumbersome.'

How many singers perform in the BBC Symphony Chorus?

'That depends on the size of the stage. At the Barbican, for
example, the maximum number that we can get on the stage
is 120. It's bigger at the Albert Hall and so the numbers tend
to go up for the Proms. Again, it depends partly on the repertoire but also in such a big space as the Albert Hall you kind
of need to see big numbers and so that is why, very often, the
Symphony Chorus will invite other choruses to join us for
a performance of, for example, *Belshazzar's Feast* or Verdi's
Requiem. So we might join forces with the BBC National

Chorus of Wales, or the London Philharmonic Chorus, or one of the other choruses that we like working with.'

So, you can have hundreds on stage?

'The Albert Hall stage is not huge, even though it's a big venue. The Albert Hall stage is not huge, even though it's a big venue. The music always comes first, but the bigger the chorus, the fewer seats there are available to sell. We will have some chorus on stage and then they will go up into the galleries behind.'

And the numbers for the BBC Singers?

'The BBC Singers has 18 full-time staff, and there are some 50–50 job shares. So we have five sopranos, four altos, four tenors and five basses.'

How long is an orchestra's rehearsal time for a prom night?

'Normally on the day of a concert we'll have a three-hour rehearsal in the morning, or in the afternoon if another orchestra is there, and we will get ready for the concert at 7.30pm or sometimes at 7pm. Occasionally we do late-night concerts. The stage crew has to work really fast to get one orchestra off and the other one on and set up.

'It might be a three-and-a-half-hour concert that you've got to rehearse in three hours. So, although we will have done two days rehearsal in the studio beforehand, we come down into the Hall and rehearse with the TV crew, which is really important, because they have to know the scores and rehearse the camera angles and know when to have a close-up on a soloist. But the team is very experienced.

They have been doing it for donkeys' years and so everybody knows what to do.'

How special is the Last Night for the players?

'It's possibly the most important gig of the year. It's the most high profile and it's also by far the most complicated concert of any we ever do, and that's because there are a lot of short pieces, you've got multiple soloists, the stage is usually packed, there's a certain expectation and it's a long concert.

'But everybody sees it as a huge honour because it's the most famous music festival in the world. It's watched by millions and listened to by millions and the Hall itself is packed. I can't think of any conductor in the 20 Proms seasons that I have been involved in who hasn't seen it as a massive honour.'

CHAPTER 3

A NEW HOME

'I have conducted through two wars, and am prepared to conduct through a third, if necessary'

– Henry Wood

KEEP CALM AND CARRY ON

At the end of the concert on 1 September 1939, Henry Wood made a brief announcement that 'the Promenade Concerts will close down until further notice'. There would be no 'Last Prom'. The following year, the Proms were again truncated when the heaviest bombing of London started during the Blitz, which saw the season end abruptly on 7 September, halfway through the intended eight-week run. Wood was also forced to find private sponsorship after the BBC pulled out of sponsorship at the outbreak of the war. The Proms continued, nonetheless, throughout the Second World War. The BBC Orchestra was replaced by the London Symphony Orchestra, backed by the Royal Philharmonic Society, before the BBC returned in 1942.

BLITZED

At around 11pm on 10 May 1941, hours after an afternoon performance of Elgar's *The Dream of Gerontius* conducted by Malcolm Sargent, a bomb hit the roof of the Queen's Hall during a heavy Luftwaffe night raid.

Two firewatchers quickly started putting out the flames with hoses after the bomb set the roof alight. They thought they had successfully managed to put out the fire, but a little while later the roof reignited and was soon engulfed by flames. The Auxiliary Fire Service struggled to cope with the many fires in London on a night that also saw the House of Commons, Westminster Abbey and the British Museum hit by bombs, and they ran out of water.

The following morning, the roof of this magnificent building had fallen in and the remains of the grand organ was a pitiful mess of charred wood and molten metal.

Henry Wood was photographed, looking noble in his three-piece suit and bow tie, hat in hand, atop the rubble. His defiant response to the tragedy was: 'We must build another Queen's Hall.'

Wood's indominatable spirit and 'stiff upper lip' was symbolised when the bronze bust of the conductor was unearthed from the ashes – practically the only thing to have survived completely undamaged. It seemed like an omen.

'You never heard him say "We can't do without Queen's Hall." You did hear him say, "We must build another Queen's Hall."'

– Lady Jessie Wood, recalling the words of her partner, Henry Wood

BRONZE BUST

The bronze bust of Henry Wood that was found in the rubble of the old Queen's Hall was made by Donald Gilbert in 1936 and had been unveiled there in September 1938. It was donated to the Royal Academy of Music by Lady Jessie Wood in 1955 on condition that it would be taken from the Duke's Hall each year to the BBC Proms in the Royal Albert Hall. This tradition has been carried out ever since. Today, someone from the BBC Live Events team will go to collect the bust from the Royal Academy and bring it to the Albert Hall in a taxi. One of the crew then lifts it onto the podium where Sir Henry can look down on the audience from his lofty position behind the orchestra. The bust is adorned with a laurel chaplet on the Last Night of the Proms.

A NEW BEGINNING

The only other venue in London capable of managing large-scale orchestral concerts was the grand Royal Albert Hall, which could hold an audience twice the size of that which the Queen's Hall had been able to accommodate. The 47th Proms began here on 12 July 1941, lasting six weeks.

Wood ended the first prom promptly at 9pm in order to allow people to get home before the night's blackout.

This rule was enforced for all performances until the end of the war. There was no wailing siren to interrupt the orchestra, but a red light was shown in the auditorium if an air raid was imminent and evacuation was advisable. Undaunted, most devoted Prommers remained, wrapped up in the wonderful music and willing to take their chances!

STONEY STARES

As well as Wood's bronze bust, five Portland stone busts from the façade of the Queen's Hall were recovered, those of Beethoven, Mozart, Bach, Haydn and probably, but not definitely, Purcell. They are housed at the Royal Academy of Music, where they stand on plinths in the foyer of the Josefowitz Recital Hall.

THE FIRST LAST NIGHT IN A NEW HOME

Henry Wood conducted the London Symphony Orchestra at the first Last Night at the Royal Albert Hall on 23 August 1941. The programme included a mix of contemporary and traditional music as usual and the finale of Wood's own *Fantasia on British Sea-Songs*, followed by the national anthem.

At the end of the first Last Night performance at the Royal Albert Hall, Henry Wood gave the first proper 'Conductor's Speech', which was set to become a familiar tradition. Wood had avoided speaking to the audiences up to that point, partly because he was a shy man and partly because he felt it would highlight his upper-class background and detract from the inclusive message of the Proms. The speech came as a complete surprise to the delighted audience, as it was in marked contrast to Wood's usual exit, when he conducted the encores and then put on his hat and coat and departed. Instead, he turned to the audience and thanked his sponsors and the Prommers, without whom the season would not have been able to go ahead in its new home. Despite problems with the acoustics in the Royal Albert Hall, which resulted in an echo, and comments in the newspapers about the less 'homely' atmosphere of the new venue, the season was judged to be a success.

The following year, having set a precedent by thanking those who had helped make the concerts happen as well as those who enjoyed them, Wood once again turned to the audience at the end of the Last Night and acknowledged those listening on the wireless, as well as praising the Promenaders. The audience cheered wildly when he added, 'How you listen!' He said it had been a 'glorious season' and he looked forward to meeting them all next year in what he hoped would be 'days of peace'. The applause went on and on. For a quarter of an hour the audience cheered and sang 'For He's a Jolly Good Fellow' – all broadcast live on BBC radio.

MAKING PLANS

Wood was so pleased with the transition to the new home that on 1 August 1941, just three weeks into the first season there, he wrote a letter entitled '1942 Promenade Concerts', requesting that arrangements be made for the Proms to continue at the Royal Albert Hall the following year. It read:

Dear Mr. Askew,

I should like to feel that my Promenade Concerts will find a home here next year, and with this in view, I shall be glad if you will allow me to pencil the Hall as from approximately July 11th to August 22nd, or should conditions allow, then a further two weeks to September 5th.

I am very happy to have had this my 47th season in the Royal Albert Hall and take this opportunity of thanking you for all you have done to assist me, via your Staff. I could not have believed I could settle down so happily away from my old home at Queen's Hall.

Sincerely yours,
Henry J. Wood.

THE ROYAL ALBERT HALL

The Great Exhibition of 1851 took place in a purpose-built Crystal Palace in London's Hyde Park. Organised by influential civil servant Henry Cole and Prince Albert, it successfully promoted the arts, manufacturing and commerce. Prince Albert was so pleased with it that he later proposed a permanent building for the advancement of the arts and sciences. However, he died in 1861 without seeing his idea come to fruition.

A memorial to Prince Albert was proposed for Hyde Park with a great hall opposite that would home and display arts and sciences. The building was designed by two civil engineers, Francis Fowke and Henry Scott, who were influenced by the impressive amphitheatres of ancient Rome. It was to be built by the Lucas Brothers.

On 20 May 1867, at a special ceremony in a vast marquee, Queen Victoria laid a red Aberdeen granite foundation stone using a golden trowel. She also inserted a glass 'time-capsule' underneath it containing an inscription and a collection of gold and silver coins. It has never been retrieved and what the inscription says is unknown. The stone is partially visible underneath seat 87 in K stalls, row 11. Take a look if you ever sit there!

During the ceremony, the queen surprised everyone by announcing that the name of the building was to be changed from the Central Hall of Arts and Sciences. Instead, in memory of her beloved Bertie, she announced it would be called the Royal Albert Hall of Arts and Sciences.

Over 7,000 people attended the ceremony. A composition by Prince Albert, 'Invocation to Harmony', was performed by an orchestra conducted by Michael Costa. A 21-gun salute was fired in Hyde Park and there was a trumpet fanfare.

'It is my wish that this Hall should bear
his name to whom it will have owed its
existence and be called the Royal Albert
Hall of Arts and Sciences'

– **Queen Victoria, speaking at the laying ceremony**

THE FRIEZE

The distinctive mosaic frieze that encircles the building
is 800 feet long and formed of foot-long slabs of mosaic
tesserae depicting the advancement of the arts and sciences
of all nations. Terracotta letters are inscribed 12 inches
(300mm) high about the frieze, combining historical and
religious quotations. It reads:

'This Hall was erected for the advancement of
the Arts & Sciences and works of industry of all
nations in fulfilment of the intention of Albert
Prince Consort. The site was purchased with the
proceeds of the Great Exhibition of the year
MDCCCLI. The first stone of the Hall was laid
by Her Majesty Queen Victoria on the twentieth
day of May MDCCCLXVII and it was opened by
Her Majesty the twenty ninth of March in the year
MDCCCLXXI. Thine O Lord is the greatness and
the power and the glory and the victory and the
majesty for all that is in the heaven and in the earth

is thine. The wise and their works are in the hand of God. Glory be to God on high and on Earth peace.'

THE DOME

Designed by Rowland Mason Ordish and constructed by Fairbairn Engineering Company, the dome is made of wrought iron and glazed. A trial assembly took place at the Fairbairn site at Ardwick, near Manchester. It was then taken apart again and transported to London by horse and cart and successfully reassembled onto the rest of the building on 11 May 1869.

FILLING THE HALL

The audience capacity for the Royal Albert Hall today is 6,000 in total. Of this, 900 can stand in the arena and 500 in the gallery, with the remaining 4,600 seated.

OFFICIAL OPENING

Following the laying of the foundation stone, work continued on the building over the following years, and it was officially opened by Queen Victoria and Edward, Prince of Wales, on 29 March 1871.

A concert followed and there was immediate concern about the acoustics. Engineers later tried to fix the strong echo caused by the curve of the ceiling by suspending a canvas awning below the dome. But although it was of some benefit, the problem continued. The awning was removed in 1949 and fluted aluminium panels were installed below the roof, but the echo could not be eradicated.

THE MUSHROOMS

Following acoustic tests carried out in the late sixties, the suspending of fibreglass acoustic diffusers from the roof was recommended. This resulted in the much-loved Jules Verne fantasy-like 'mushrooms' hanging from the ceiling like mysterious underwater creatures.

Originally 135 mushrooms were made by the Yorkshire Fibreglass Company, which were fitted in 1969. Sir William Glock, Controller of BBC Music, triumphantly wrote in the 1969 Proms Guide, 'The acoustics have been transformed. The famous echo has become past history.'

Advanced testing in 2001 led to 50 diffusers being removed and the remaining 85 reconfigured. There is now a greater density of mushrooms in the centre of the ceiling and above and behind the stage, where they had not been previously placed. This further improved the quality of the sound for the audience.

GRAND SOUND

The Grand Organ in the Royal Albert Hall is the second-largest pipe organ in Britain. Originally built by Henry 'Father' Willis in 1871, it was rebuilt by Mander Organs in 2002–2004 and was the largest in the UK until 2007, when its record was broken by Liverpool Anglican Cathedral. It has 147 stops and 9,999 pipes with a total length of nine miles.

THE MEMORIAL

The original idea for a memorial commemorating the Great Exhibition of 1851 was for the plinth to bear a statue of Britannia. But following the death of Prince Albert, Queen Victoria arranged for a statue of her late husband to stand on top instead.

It was installed in 1863 in the Royal Horticultural Society Gardens in Brompton. After the gardens were closed in 1882, it was relocated to its present location opposite the Hall's south entrance on the Queen Elizabeth II Diamond Jubilee Steps.

TOUCHING AUDIENCE

The Director of the BBC Proms, David Pickard, thinks that a combination of venue and long history is what make the Proms so special ...

'Part of the public interest in the Proms comes from their longevity. I mean, 1895 was a very long while ago and the Proms are still going strong. I think that people are aware that each Proms season represents another part of the development of the festival. I think also for the Proms there is no doubt that the atmosphere in the Albert Hall is something that is unique in any concert hall in the world. Certainly, in my experience, when orchestras come and play at the Proms, particularly when they have never played there before, they are simply bowled over by the fact that they have this huge audience very close to them. They can almost touch the Promenaders. And yet they are also probably the most silent, concentrated audience in the world. The listening is so extraordinary there. So I think it's probably these two things that make the Proms special.'

THE BEDFORD PROMS

Prom 29 of the 1944 season, on Thursday 13 July 1944 at the Royal Albert Hall, was cancelled by the authorities owing to flying bombs known as 'doodlebugs', which had started to fall on London in June.

During 1940 and 1941 German air-raids prompted a move from the BBC Music Department's temporary home in Bristol to Bedford. Prom 29 continued, at Bedford's Corn Exchange, and was broadcast with Wood conducting.

The Proms continued to take place in Bedford for the remainder of the 1944 season, and it was here, on 28 July, that Wood conducted what was to be his final concert. He was taken ill in early August and was unable to conduct the 50th-anniversary prom on 10 August.

Adrian Boult, chief conductor of the BBC SO, and Basil Cameron took on conducting duties for the season both at the Albert Hall and Bedford Corn Exchange.

Wood died on 19 August 1944 at Hitchin Hospital, Hertfordshire. His funeral service was held in the town at St Mary's Church and his ashes were interred in the Musician's Chapel of St Sepulchre-without-Newgate in London.

TO BUILD OR NOT TO BUILD

A long debate went on about whether or not to build another Queen's Hall. Jessie Wood blamed the general post-war climate of financial hardship for the lack of funds. But, initially at least, the intention was that a new version should rise from the ashes.

There was early determination from the Treasury, who said that the site should be used for the same purpose as previously. The new Arts Council wanted a rebuilt Queen's Hall involved in the Festival of Britain of 1951. But four years later, a committee report proposed that Queen's Hall should not be rebuilt.

In 1959 there was talk about using the site to build a hotel. Finally, in 1962, a plan was drawn up to build St George's Hotel and it is this hotel that occupies the site to this day.

CHAPTER 4

BEHIND THE SCENES

'Anyone backstage will tell you I love a cake and drink endless cups of tea'

– Katie Derham, BBC TV Proms presenter

It will come as no surprise that the organisation and work that go into creating the world's biggest music festival constitute a mammoth undertaking. Everyone plays their role, from the initial ideas and plans to selling ice cream on the night. And what makes the Proms especially tricky to run smoothly is that, by their nature, they continue to evolve and spread with new innovations every year.

Let's take a walk behind the scenes to get an idea of who does what, when and where and how!

THE GUV'NOR

The Director of the BBC Proms is the spearhead of the whole operation, planning for months and years ahead, and overseeing the programme and the arrangements over the whole season.

Current director David Pickard admits to being terrified when he took over the position for his first season in 2016. He was thankful for inheriting a brilliant team and for personally knowing his predecessors to whom he could go for advice.

How daunting was it when you first took the reins?
'It was terrifying because you look back at all your predecessors, all of whom I have admired immensely for what they delivered and contributed to the Proms, and it's a daunting task to follow in their footsteps. But, of course, it's also a huge privilege because you have the greatest classical music festival in the world in your hands to create what you want to out of it.'

What does your own job entail in organising it?
'My job in the Proms is really one of artistic planning. So I am the person who effectively decides what appears in each concert and how the whole season flows. I am the artistic director but, having said that, the way that it works is that the people that contribute to those plans are the artists themselves. So whilst I may have an overview of what I would like the whole of the Proms to contain, and I have the ultimate decision as to what we play and when and with whom, all the various participants bring their own ideas, their own enthusiasms and their own vision to the concerts they perform in.'

Did any of your predecessors in the role give you advice?
'I have had lots of advice from various people but, I have to say, only when I have asked for it, and it's been very helpful. But each of us who have been director of the Proms do it in our own individual way. We all have our own different particular priorities and that is part of the evolution of the Proms. A new person comes in and takes over and does things slightly differently.'

*Can you give us an example of a good piece of advice
that has been passed on?*

'One piece of advice that I was given by Nick Kenyon
[Director of the BBC Proms 1996–2007], which I thought
was very interesting, was, "You have to get used to saying
'no'." And what he meant by that was that there is so much
on offer for the Proms, there are so many things to choose
from, that inevitably you are disappointing people because
there is never enough space for all the things you want to do.'

*Before taking up your role you were General Director of
Glyndebourne. Was that a help when it came to the Proms?*

'I think it was a help in the sense that I was used to giving
up my summers! I haven't had a summer holiday in 20
years. But actually, although the two may seem very different, there are remarkable similarities, because they are both
events as well as festivals, so going to Glyndebourne isn't
just like an ordinary night at the opera and going to the
Proms isn't just like an ordinary night at the concert hall.
They have a very distinctive atmosphere to them, which
goes beyond the music that is being performed.'

Where are you on the night of each prom?

'I am backstage before the concert because I try to go
round everybody and wish them good luck, and then I run
up to a box in the grand tier, where Alan Davey [Controller
of BBC Radio 3] and I are very often entertaining guests
and watching and enjoying the Proms. So, I've seen every
single prom since the beginning of 2016 and I don't intend
to spoil that record.

'It's a funny thing, at Glyndebourne, where you might have a run of 15 performances of an opera, I felt that I could take the odd night off, but with the Proms, when every single concert is unique and you've invested a lot of energy and time and thought and emotion into each one, you want to see how they all turn out. And I always watch out front.

'I'm told that William Glock [BBC Controller of the Proms 1959–73] never stayed in the Albert Hall. He used to just go home and listen to it all on the radio because he thought his job was done.'

How do you narrow down who you choose to be in each concert?

'There are certain formulas to do with the way the Proms are planned. We have these wonderful BBC orchestras, so it makes sense for us that they have a share of the Proms. So the BBC Symphony Orchestra, BBC National Orchestra of Wales, BBC Scottish Symphony Orchestra, BBC Philharmonic, BBC Concert Orchestra and BBC Singers all have an allocation of Proms each summer. There are then other really important UK orchestras that we like to try to feature on an annual basis, and we have a lot of glamorous international orchestras that want to come to the Proms as well. That is what that makes the Proms so distinctive, that you can come and hear the Berlin Philharmonic or the Vienna Philharmonic or any of the great orchestras in the world. There will be a selection of those at the Proms every year. And then of course there are the new orchestras that have sprung up. In 2018 we have got four or five orchestras who have never appeared at the Proms, and we keep renewing and refreshing the people that we ask to come and play.'

MAKING CHANGES

William Glock, Director of the BBC Proms from 1959 to 1973, was keen to make changes to the planning stages as soon as he took charge.

'When I arrived at the BBC I found that the Proms were planned by committee. The idea seemed to be that you looked at the previous year's programmes and just made a few changes. No question of starting with a blank sheet. I knew this would have to stop.

'I don't think any serious activities can be managed by committees. They simply can't achieve great things. You need one person's vision. I could have made what was then a radical new idea, such as including a Bach "Passion", and someone would have vetoed it.'

THE BULL RUN

To reach the stage, artists and musicians walk along a narrow tunnel that leads from an underground corridor into the arena of the Albert Hall. This well-trodden route is known as the 'bull run'. Emerging into the blazing lights of the arena, full of the massed, expectant faces of the audience, can be a startling experience.

'Going out there is like getting a huge shot of adrenalin,' recalled Roger Wright, BBC Proms Director from 2007 to 2014. 'The atmosphere hits you. Although it can be noisy when you arrive on stage, it becomes magically still when the performance is about to begin.'

Wright would be backstage, dispensing encouragement to those about to walk the bull run. To newcomers he would pass on advice that other artists had told him – not to be put off by the proximity to the audience.

'If people can get as enthusiastic about music as about football, that is all to the good'

– Malcolm Sargent, conductor

A TAX-ING DAY

Mezzo-soprano Sarah Walker's first Last Night appearance as a singer was a dramatic one that made her extra anxious.

'My first Last Night was particularly difficult because I already had a previous engagement in London performing at the Wigmore Hall with the Nash Ensemble, so they very kindly rearranged their programme so that the piece I was singing with them was in the first half of the programme. A taxi was waiting for me outside the back door, and I jumped in and raced over to the Albert Hall. Now, that would have been OK, but I also had a heavy cold and I knew that I really should not have done one of those two concerts. But you don't give up the Last Night of the Proms, and it would have been insensitive and unprofessional to "cry off" the other one. So I just did them, which probably meant that you could barely hear me in the Albert Hall itself, although it sounded fine on the radio. I was nervous because I didn't feel I could do it justice.'

TEA AND TANGERINE TIME

Says singer Bryn Terfel:

'On a given night at the Proms, you are always there in the afternoon to rehearse, so that is your warming-up routine in a nutshell. Usually there are a couple of hours between the end of the rehearsal and the Royal Albert Hall filling up with people, so there is not much time. I'll maybe have a cup of tea or a tangerine or two. That is usually how I prepare before the actual concert begins. Nothing ground-breaking that somebody can steal and put in a bottle!'

MAKING EVENTS HAPPEN

Helen Heslop, who is the manager of the Live Events team from the BBC Proms and Radio 3, has been right in the thick of things for 22 seasons. From the planning process to the overseeing of the event on the night, Helen is there to make sure everything works and runs to schedule.

What does your job entail?
'There are two sides to my job. I work on the artistic planning at the Proms with David Pickard, the Director of the BBC Proms, and run the backstage operation. My amazing team makes the events run smoothly for the live audience as well as keeping the radio and TV broadcasts in mind. In other words, we have to run events that work for TV and radio.'

So that's everything from booking the artist to overseeing stage direction?
'Yes it is. It's quite a big job!'

Do you start planning the next Proms the minute you've finished the last?
'When we are working on the current year we are also planning two years ahead, so it's a year-round process. We are predominantly Proms, but we also work on other live events in the Radio 3 calendar. Again, we work alongside

the Radio 3 production team to ensure the events happen smoothly for broadcast and live audiences.'

How big is your team?
'There are four permanent members plus a six-month seasonal post from the end of March. It's a small core team, but I have freelancers who come in to help run backstage for some of the concerts. There are thirteen of us in total.'

What have been your biggest Last Night challenges over the years?
'One of the biggest challenges is running the concert to time. The first half is taken on BBC Two and the second half on BBC One, and it's always quite tight. If the first half starts overrunning we can't delay the start of the second half, so it means a squeezed interval. The wonderful Royal Albert Hall team then has to turn the hall around faster. It can get quite hairy.'

Have you had any near disasters?
'Over the years we have had times when the screens have malfunctioned either in rehearsal or during the link-ups to the parks. We've had artists arriving late for rehearsal and problems with microphones. The biggest near-disaster was when the building had to be evacuated and checked by the relevant authorities, which lasted a few hours. Luckily the orchestra had already rehearsed that morning and we were all allowed back into the building with enough time to make the concert happen. Generally things have run pretty smoothly!'

You must breathe a big sigh of relief when it all goes well.
'Absolutely! But the best place to be is backstage on the Last Night because it is just so exciting to be involved with the artists and the whole buzz of the event. The camaraderie between the artists is amazing. Even the big names can get nervous, and we are there to help them through it. I still get excited after all these years. I absolutely love it.'

ON YER BIKE

Bryn Terfel, who has sung on two Last Nights to date, keeps the big theatrical stage entrance for the performance itself. His arrival at the Royal Albert Hall is rather more humble – although it still manages to cause a stir …

'I have had a little apartment in Kensington since the early 1980s, so it's a very local job for me, and I go there on my bike. It takes me five minutes to get to the Royal Albert Hall and I park my bike by the stage door and the Promenaders have a good laugh about that because I am usually in my shorts. After the performance there is always a little party and then I trickle home on my bicycle.'

THE STAGE

The stage at the Royal Albert Hall is neither square nor rectangular. At its widest point it measures 24.02m and at the deepest point it is 14.53m. But it can be extended to accommodate bigger orchestras and choirs, or to create more performance space.

IN TUNE WITH THE MUSIC

Ulrich Gerhartz, Director, Concert and Artists Services, Steinway & Sons, London, is in charge of the beautiful pianos installed for the Proms, from maintenance to tuning. He arrives when it is dark and leaves when it is dark. And sometimes he even manages to relax and enjoy the music!

What is your background?

'I did an apprenticeship as a piano maker at the Steinway factory in Hamburg between 1986 and 1990, where I made new pianos. Then I transferred to Steinway in London as a freshly trained young piano maker and I went into servicing and rebuilding old Steinway pianos. And then from 1992 I transferred to Steinway Hall in London and joined the concert department, and have been involved as a piano technician with the Proms since 1992.'

Do you have to be able to play the piano to be able to do your job?

'You have to be able to play well as far as playing the keyboard evenly is concerned. The job is not to perform. The job is to be very analytical with your touch and with your ears to be able to regulate pianos to "speak" very evenly with the widest dynamic range.'

Apart from the Proms, what do you do for the rest of the year?

'At Steinway Hall, where I am based, there is a bank of eleven concert grands and four smaller ones that form our concert fleet. Out of this concert fleet come the pianos that are supplied for the Proms. They hire them from us. They are selected and looked after by me, and every season prepared for their little summer holiday in the Albert Hall.'

How many pianos do you supply for the Proms?

'We always have two concert grands permanently at the Albert Hall. One we call the solo piano, i.e. the piano used for the piano concertos, and the other one is the orchestral piano that is played as part of the orchestra. And then we have another piano teed up for the Proms that is used for what we call prepared piano, i.e. for modern pieces where the piano is modified to create different sounds. We also have another couple of concert grands lined up that play at a higher pitch for overseas orchestras that don't play at 440 hertz to the middle A. They play at a pitch from 442 to 445.'

What is a typical day for you during the Proms season?

'During the Proms the first tuning is early in the morning for either the orchestral piano or the solo piano for the morning rehearsal. The Albert Hall is quite chilly when I arrive because usually they put the chillers on so that the Hall doesn't get too hot. Occasionally I meet the pianist to discuss the piano. After that I go back to Steinway Hall to do whatever is to be done there and then return to the Albert Hall usually towards the end of the day, around 5pm, to do the tuning before the arena opens. I attend the concert until the piano-playing is finished.'

The Promenaders have a traditional joke when the middle A is played for tuning purposes, don't they?

'There is always great excitement when the piano is moved to concerto position. The Albert Hall staff lift the piano lid and you get the famous shout of "Heave" from the arena and the reply "Ho" from the gallery. The concertmaster [lead violin] then gets up to play the orchestra the middle A for the orchestra to tune to, and again there is a huge round of applause.'

How many pianos do you tune in one day at the Proms?

'Usually two tunings at the Proms, but I might do others back at Steinway or elsewhere because my responsibility is for our pianos wherever they may be at London and major UK venues. My summer is always extremely busy and divided between the Proms and the Edinburgh Festival, and also looking after and maintaining the pianos.'

Are you the sole tuner at the Proms?

'No, but I oversee everything. I decide which pianos to put in. I maintain the pianos but I work with a team of six tuners in London and the work is shared out between us. Usually we have a pre-Proms meeting and we will look through who is playing what. Some pianists will request at the Proms that I look after them but it is all finely orchestrated and it's a team effort.'

What makes a piano suitable for the Proms?

'You can have a piano that sounds lovely and sweet and beautiful and you put it on stage at the Albert Hall with an orchestra and you can't hear it. One of the biggest briefs for the Proms is that the pianos have a good-quality tone but at the same time have a tone that can project into a 6,000-seater auditorium and be heard over the orchestra.'

How long does it take you to tune one piano?

'If you tune a piano from beginning to end and raise the pitch rate from 440 to 442, it would take up to two hours to make stable. In reality, we don't get ever get more than half an hour of peace and quiet to tune at the Albert Hall. So we take pianos to the Proms that have already been tuned at a higher pitch. This means that the tuning time, whilst the Proms are going on, is anything between 15 minutes and 45 minutes. The tuning done after rehearsal is a fine tuning rather than a full one.

'Throughout the Proms season I go to the Albert Hall when it is dark in the morning and do maintenance, which means they will put both pianos on stage and I've got four hours to make sure they are clean, that nothing is broken and the pitch is all right so that when the tuner comes in they can do a fine tuning in 15 minutes.'

Do the pianos ever get damaged?

'We have had damage and that usually gets repaired on site. If it is really bad damage it will be repaired when the pianos come back to Steinway Hall after the Proms.

'It's mostly case damage because there is limited storage at the Albert Hall. The pianos live under the risers with scaffolding and stage equipment. Needless to say they do occasionally get damaged going in and out of the Hall.

We try to fix them straight away because people do notice, particularly when the Proms are televised. And if there is a chunk out of the piano it would not look very good.'

What equipment do you carry with you to do maintenance and tuning on a piano?

'The tool case carried around by piano technicians is very similar to a tuner's tool case a hundred years ago. There is very little modern technology involved. There are many adjustments you do to a piano. You tune to the scale and make sure everything is in order. Then there's 'voicing', influencing the quality of the tone and making sure that all the notes have the same dynamic range. For that you carry voicing needles that allow you to distribute the hammer head to make the note softer or brighter. We also carry hammer hardener, so if a note is too soft you can apply a lotion to make the hammer harder and the tone brighter. Then you have powder to address friction. There are lots of moving parts in the piano action and keyboard, and if there is any stiffness you have potions like Teflon powder or a Teflon-based fluid to free up sluggish centre pins or get less friction into leathers and felts. And then you have a whole range of funny-looking regulation tools with which you adjust the action of the piano mechanically if necessary.'

Do you sit at the concerts listening to the pitch of the piano or do you enjoy the music?

'If you have a very good day and you get enough time to tune and you know everything is as good as it can be and the pianist is happy, then you can enjoy the whole concert. If you haven't had enough time or you are slightly anxious about the climate in the hall or the pianist is on edge, then you are on edge as well.

'But there is a fantastic atmosphere at the Albert Hall and there's always an excitement seeing the pianist playing a concerto in a massive hall like that. It really does give you goose pimples.'

When you listen to music for relaxation, are you able to tell if the piano is out of tune and does it drive you mad?
Yes, and I would switch it off! I listen to music particularly when I am driving, because then I am undisturbed. But, of course, because of my profession I listen to the quality of the piano and how it is prepared and how it is played. That comes with the job.'

KEY TO SUCCESS

A Steinway grand piano, such as those used at the Royal Albert Hall, is three years in the making. The wood is dried and seasoned for two years before the instrument is meticulously hand-crafted, taking about 12 months.

A larger concert grand is 274cm in length, 157cm in width and weighs approximately 480kg (1,058lbs). A single concert grand retails for £140,000.

'The concerts are rehearsed concert by concert, so they start a couple of days before the First Night of the Proms. One Proms concert gets, on average, either two or three days of rehearsal. The total rehearsal being six hours'

— Sakari Oramo, Chief Conductor, BBC Symphony Orchestra

A CAPTIVE AUDIENCE

Veteran Proms conductor Sir Andrew Davis got the shock of his life for his final Last Night in 2000:

'It was an extraordinary day because we had a rehearsal in the morning and then the TV presenter Michael Aspel turned up with a camera crew and said, "Sir Andrew Davis, This Is Your Life." And they carted me off to BBC Television Centre, which was all very well but I have a routine before going on stage at the Albert Hall. There will be an orchestra rehearsal in the morning, then lunch and I'll take a nap and get quietly ready for the show. So my routine was completely messed up.

'But *This Is Your Life* turned out to be an extraordinary, moving occasion. A lot of old friends, including school friends, appeared and others sent video messages. They were all very important people from my life. And at the end, the last person to come on was Terry Waite. And I thought, "Why is he here?" I had never met him.

'He was imprisoned for years in Beirut and went through the most extraordinarily difficult situation, and he told the story of how, after months and months of requesting it, they gave him a radio. And the first thing that he heard was a BBC prom and it was Elgar's *The Dream of Gerontius* with me conducting. And he described what an incredible and very important moment it was in his life. We were all weeping in the studio by the end of it.

'It was a very emotional afternoon and then I had to go to the Last Night. It was a hell of a day!'

CHAPTER 5

THE CROWD PLEASERS

'I remember the first time I presented the Last Night of the Proms and the atmosphere in the hall was electric, as it has been every year since. You can feel the excitement in the air, and that feeling is very inclusive and upbeat'

– Katie Derham, BBC TV Proms presenter

The Last Night wouldn't be the same without staunch favourites such as 'Land of Hope and Glory', 'Jerusalem' and 'Rule, Britannia!'. This is where the Prommers really get involved with mass clapping, honking of horns and even crying!

If you want to be a true part of the action, you have to 'feel' it like an actor does a role in a drama. So here's an in-depth look at what the tunes are really about and how Prommers can be part of the performance.

FANTASIA ON BRITISH SEA-SONGS

Sir Henry Wood's nautical arrangement always provokes an eruption of activity from the Prommers, who feel their sea legs the moment the opening notes are played.

Arranged in 1905 to mark the centenary of the 1805 Battle of Trafalgar in which the Royal Navy engaged the combined fleets of the French and Spanish in what was to become known as the Napoleonic Wars, the song tells the story of the sea battle from the point of view of a British sailor.

The original 'Fantasia', first performed by Henry Wood and the Queen's Hall Orchestra at a Promenade Concert on 21 October 1905, was composed of nine parts, each marking a notable event on the voyage from beginning to end. Usually just a selection is performed on the Last Night, which has varied over the years. The 2017 Proms, for instance, featured 'The Saucy Arethusa', 'Tom Bowling', 'Jack's the Lad (Hornpipe)', 'See, the Conqu'ring Hero Comes' and, of course, 'Rule, Britannia!'.

Here are the stories behind the full version of the airs …

1. 'BUGLE CALLS'

The six calls, conveying orders and their responses aboard a naval ship, are in sequence: Admiral's Salute, Action, General Assembly, Landing Party, Prepare to Ram, and Quick, Double, Extend and Close.

2. 'THE ANCHOR'S WEIGHED'

This hopeful and inspiring section marks the beginning of the journey, as the anchor is raised and the mighty ship sets sail. Thoughts turn to what lies ahead as the adventure begins. The tune has a melancholy air to it, with trombones and trumpets to the fore, bringing to mind the ship gliding away from shore, gradually picking up speed as it heads towards an unknown fate.

3. 'THE SAUCY ARETHUSA'

The origins of this are somewhat complicated, but this hornpipe commemorates a battle between the British frigate HMS *Arethusa* and the French ship *Belle Poule* during the American Revolutionary War, and not the Napoleonic Wars. The *Arethusa* (named after the water nymph of Greek mythology) was built in 1757 and purchased by the French navy, from whom she was captured by the British in 1759. After the French allied with America and entered the American Revolutionary War in 1778, a British fleet intercepted four French ships on 17 June of that year, who were on a reconnaissance mission in the English Channel. A warning shot across the bows was returned with canon fire and a battle broke out – the first between British and French naval forces during the American Revolutionary War. The *Arethusa* lost her main mast and was forced to withdraw. The *Belle Poule* lost 30 men and her second captain before getting away.

The French claimed it as a great victory and women of the French court revelled in an outlandish new hairstyle called 'à la *Belle Poule*', made popular by Marie Antoinette. It comprised piles of powdered and curled hair that was stretched over a wooden frame and then decorated with a model of the ship, complete with flags and sails!

But the British too decided to claim the battle as a victory. Englishman Prince Hoare wrote a poem, 'The Arethusa', to commemorate the battle, with a decidedly English spin on the events. In 1796 this text was combined with a melody that had been composed back in 1725 by

Irish harper Turlough O'Carolan, originally known as 'Miss MacDermott' or 'Princess Royal'. It formed part of William Shield's small opera, *The Lock and Key*. This fiddle air was taken by Sir Henry Wood for *Fantasia on British Sea-Songs*.

Coiffure *à la Belle-Poule*, 1778
© Heritage Image Partnership Ltd/Alamy

THE REAL ARETHUSA

In Greek mythology Arethusa was a water nymph and the daughter of Nereus who came from the underwater world of Arcadia. Her beauty attracted the amorous attentions of the river god Alpheus but, wanting to stay chaste to serve the goddess Artemis, she fled his advances.

Artemis hid her in a cloud but Alpheus persisted. Paralysed with fear, Arethusa began to perspire and eventually turned into an underground stream, breaking ground to become a freshwater fountain on the island of Ortygia, in Syracuse, Sicily. Undeterred, Alpheus flowed through the sea to mingle with Arethusa's waters.

4. 'TOM BOWLING'

The lament, signifying the death aboard ship of a British sailor, Tom Bowling, was written by Charles Dibdin, a British composer, musician, dramatist, novelist and actor. In 1788 his beloved eldest brother, Thomas Dibdin, captain of a ship in the East India trade, had invited him to visit Charles in India. But before he could get there, Thomas died at sea.

A heartbroken Dibdin wrote 'Tom Bowling' in memory of him. A sentimental song, also known as 'The Sailor's

Epitaph', it was first performed in the entertainment The Oddities at The Lyceum in 1789. The first verse sets the tone:

> Here a sheer hulk lies poor Tom Bowling,
> The darling of our crew;
> No more he'll hear the tempest howling,
> For death has broach'd him to.
> His form was of the manliest beauty,
> His heart was kind and soft.
> Faithful, below, he did his duty.
> But now he's gone aloft.

CHARLES DIBDIN

Born to a 50-year-old mother in Southampton in 1740, Charles Dibdin was the 18th son of a poor silvermaker. He began his musical career as a boy, becoming a celebrated chorister at Winchester Cathedral, before moving to London to stay with a brother and working as a harpsichord tuner. He wrote his first operetta at the age of 22, whilst working as a singer and actor in Covent Garden, and became the resident composer there in 1778.

In 1803 the British government commissioned him to write a series of songs to 'keep alive the national feelings against the French', for which he was paid £200 a year, the equivalent of £16,500 today. It was said his patriotic songs were worth 'ten thousand sailors' to the English cause.

Despite his success, Dibdin died in poverty in Camden Town on 25 July 1814. He was buried in St Martin's churchyard under a headstone inscribed with four lines of 'Tom Bowling'.

5. 'JACK'S THE LAD (HORNPIPE)'

Life must go on and, after the sad tale of Tom Bowling, the crew of the *Arethusa* listen to a jaunty sailor's hornpipe to raise their spirits.

Hornpipes were traditionally danced to in bare feet. Also known as 'The Sailor's Hornpipe' and 'The College Hornpipe', the melody is thought to have been written on Tyneside circa 1770. The dance imitates the life of a sailor and his duties aboard ship, particularly the hauling of ropes, looking out to sea, climbing the rigging and saluting.

Captain Cook ordered his men to dance the hornpipe as a way to keep them in good health whilst at sea. The musical accompaniment would be a tin whistle, squeezebox or fiddle, or any combination of these three.

6. 'FAREWELL AND ADIEU, YE SPANISH LADIES'

Time to slow things down with some melancholy trombones for this traditional British naval song describing a voyage home from Spain.

Also known simply as 'Spanish Ladies', it was thought to have been written between 1793 and 1796, when the Royal Navy carried supplies to Spain to aid its resistance to revolutionary France. It was a farewell lament sung on board the homebound ship as a tribute to the exotic Spanish women they had seen or met. It became a favourite sea shanty among sailors as they raised the anchor to return home from any far-flung voyage.

The lyrics begin:

Farewell and adieu to you, Spanish ladies,
Farewell and adieu to you, ladies of Spain;
For we have received orders
For to sail to old England,
But we hope in a short time to see you again.

At the Proms just the tune is played, without lyrics.

Fans of the movie *Jaws* may recall Robert Shaw's character, Quint, singing a wry version of 'Spanish Ladies' to Richard Dreyfuss's character, oceanographer Hooper, after being shown his 'anti-shark cage'.

Farewell and adieu to you, fair Spanish ladies,
Farewell and adieu, you ladies of Spain;
For I've received orders
For to sail back to Boston,
And so nevermore shall we see you again.

7. 'HOME, SWEET HOME'

With the battle won, it's time to turn for home.

Beginning with a solo clarinet, the tune goes into the familiar refrain, instantly recognisable by its alternative title 'There's No Place Like Home'. The melody was penned by English composer Henry Bishop with words by American lyricist John Howard Payne for an opera that was first produced in London in 1823. It became hugely popular in America and was a favourite of both Union and Confederate soldiers during the American Civil War.

The first verse:

Mid pleasures and palaces
Though I may roam
Be it ever so humble
There's no place like home.

8. 'SEE, THE CONQU'RING HERO COMES'

Triumphant trumpets followed by French horns proclaim a stirring victory anthem as our naval heroes are feted on their return home. It was composed in 1747 by George Frideric Handel for his oratorio *Joshua*, with lyrics by Thomas Morell. Due to its popularity it was later inserted into a revival of Handel's earlier oratorio, *Judas Maccabaeus*.

9. 'RULE, BRITANNIA!'

Finally, to underline how Britain will continue to 'rule the waves', the 'Fantasia' ends with the rousing rendition of 'Rule, Britannia!'.

The song, sung by a leading singer – usually a soprano – with a triumphant chorus from the audience, is the ultimate expression of patriotism. Originated from the poem 'Rule, Britannia' by Scottish poet and playwright James Thomson, it was set to music by Thomas Arne in 1740 and formed part of the masque *Alfred*, about Alfred the Great, co-written by Thomson and David Mallet.

Masques were a popular form of entertainment in sixteenth- and seventeenth-century England, involving verse and masks. *Alfred* was first performed on 1 August 1740 at Cliveden, the country home of Frederick, Prince of Wales, the eldest son of George II, to commemorate his accession and the third birthday of his daughter, Princess Augusta.

Frederick was on bad terms with his father and he sought to ingratiate himself and to further his public appeal with a masque linking him with Alfred the Great's victories over the Vikings. Featuring a dramatic pageant of poetry, music and dancing against a background of natural scenery, the masque included six songs, the last of which was 'Rule, Britannia!'. The song proved so popular that it took on an independent life of its own. The lyrics have changed a little over the years. Here is the original version published in 1763, with words in parentheses explaining the historical meaning and context:

When Britain first, at heaven's command

(Suggesting that British conquest was 'rightful' as it came from God and Brits were the 'chosen people'.)

Arose from out the azure main;

(The ocean. Azure is 'bright blue'.)

This was the charter of the land,

(God's command was to ensure certain freedoms and a Protestant political supremacy.)

And guardian angels sang this strain:

(Lauded by heaven's angels)

'Rule, Britannia! rule the waves:

(Maritime power was of vital importance and British dominance was represented by the trident that Britannia, like Neptune, wields.)

'Britons never will be slaves.'

(The British will never be subdued by a foreign power.)

Britain had the largest colonies and this song displays her feeling of superiority towards other nations. Lyricist James Thomson had previously written *The Tragedy of Sophonisba* in 1730, based on the historical figure of Sophonisba, the proud princess of Carthage, a major sea-power of the ancient world. She had committed suicide rather than submit to slavery at the hands of the Romans. This may have inspired Thomson to pen the final defiant line of 'Rule, Britannia!'.

The verse continues:

The nations, not so blest as thee,
Must, in their turns, to tyrants fall
While thou shalt flourish great and free,

The dread and envy of them all.

'Rule, Britannia! rule the waves:

'Britons never will be slaves.'

(Thomson wrote the word 'never' only once, but it developed into 'never, never, never', because it is easier to sing to the tune.)

Still more majestic shalt thou rise,

More dreadful, from each foreign stroke;

(an acknowledgement of some inevitable defeats in warfare but which only serve to make the nation rise more powerful than before)

As the loud blast that tears the skies,

Serves but to root thy native oak.

(The oak is a symbol of British history and culture as well as strength and steadfastness.)

'Rule, Britannia! rule the waves:

'Britons never will be slaves.'

All their attempts to bend thee down,

Will but arouse thy generous flame;

But work their woe, and thy renown.

'Rule, Britannia! rule the waves:

'Britons never will be slaves.'

To thee belongs the rural reign;

Thy cities shall with commerce shine:

All thine shall be the subject main,

And every shore it circles thine.

'Rule, Britannia! rule the waves:

'Britons never will be slaves.'

The Muses, still with freedom found,

(The arts can flourish through freedom and liberty.)

Shall to thy happy coast repair;
Blest Isle! With matchless beauty crown'd,
And manly hearts to guard the fair.
(Brave men will protect women.)
'Rule, Britannia! rule the waves:
'Britons never will be slaves.'

Certain words and phrases have been corrupted over the years resulting in the song invariably being sung incorrectly.

The comma after 'Rule' and before 'Britannia' is important because it signifies an exhortation to rule, not a boast. And an 's' was added to 'Rules the waves' in the Victorian era when the British did rule the waves. The Victorians also changed 'will' to a more defiant 'shall' in the line, 'Britons never shall be slaves'.

So remember, when singing along: punctuation, please!

THE BATTLE OF TRAFALGAR

In 1805 Admiral Horatio Nelson and the British fleet defeated the combined French and Spanish fleets at Cape Trafalgar, off the Spanish coast near Cadiz. The Franco-Spanish fleet lost 22 of its 33 ships whilst the 27 British ships remained intact.

Nelson was fatally wounded during the battle, but the victory (which was also the name of the ship on which he sailed) was the most decisive naval battle of the Napoleonic Wars and established Britain's supremacy on the sea.

'I found the most difficult thing about "Rule, Britannia!" was learning the verses,' said Sarah Walker, who sang at the Last Night in 1985 and again in 1989. 'We all know verse one. We probably know a bit about two, but we were doing four verses and they are totally unmemorisable. I remember saying in an interview beforehand, "What I need are idiot cards" and we laughed. Months later, I came out onto the platform at the Royal Albert Hall on the Last Night of the Proms, and there in the front row all the Prommers were standing up, each one holding a letter that together read "Idiot Cards". Unfortunately the camera doesn't show you that, but you can see from my face as I looked down how startled I was. It was lovely.'

'JERUSALEM'

English poet William Blake wrote the words to this famous verse in 1804 as a preface to his epic poem *Milton*, published in 1808. In Blake's poem, the poet Milton, author of *Paradise Lost*, comes down from heaven to earth to redeem the fallen nation, Albion.

The inspiration behind the preface poem, entitled 'And Did Those Feet in Ancient Time', was partly a medieval legend that, as a boy, Jesus of Nazareth visited England with his great uncle, Joseph of Arimathea, who was a sailor and trader. The other reference is 'the New Jerusalem' from the Bible's Book of Revelation. There it is said that one day Jesus will come back to earth to defeat Satan once and for all, ending all suffering on earth. Then he will found the New Jerusalem, which is a symbol for a kingdom of peace, love and happiness. Or, heaven on earth.

Far from the poem being a patriotic ode to England, it was deeply critical of the establishment. Blake was a social reformer, an admirer of the French Revolution, who advocated the rights of the poor and downtrodden and loathed the 'dark satanic mills' of the industrial revolution.

Blake lived in Lambeth for a while and, every time he walked into the City of London, he would have passed by the blackened and roofless shell of the Albion Flour Mills, burned down in 1791. The factory was equipped with the latest steam-powered rotary machinery that enabled the grinding of wheat night and day. But local millers were afraid of being put out of business and the factory was strongly suspected of being the target of arson. It was said local millers were seen dancing on Blackfriars Bridge in the light of the flames.

It was the poet laureate Robert Bridges who came up with the idea of setting the words to music. He asked composer Charles Hubert Parry to make 'music that an audience could take up and join in'. The result, in 1916, was a beautiful, skin-tingling anthem. But here are the true meanings behind the words ...

> And did those feet in ancient time,
> Walk upon England's mountains green?
> (Did Jesus ever walk in England?)
> And was the holy Lamb of God
> (Jesus Christ)

On England's pleasant pastures seen?

And did the Countenance Divine

Shine forth upon our clouded hills?

(Did Jesus' face light England's highest hills where he preached about love and forgiveness.)

And was Jerusalem builded here

(A metaphor for heaven)

Among these dark Satanic Mills?

(Refers to the factories of the Industrial Revolution, including the Albion Flour Mills near his home, which Blake saw as a mechanism for the enslavement of millions in unhealthy, polluted conditions – a contrast between light and dark with the previous line. An alternative interpretation is that 'mills' here may be metaphorical and instead be alluding to churches, as Blake disliked the Church of England.)

Bring me my Bow of burning gold!

Bring me my Arrows of desire!

(Bows, arrows and spears are all symbolic weapons, meaning he is ready to fight for this kingdom of justice.)

Bring me my Spear: O clouds unfold!

(Beseeching the clouds to disperse so that one can see the sky clearly.)

Bring me my Chariot of fire!

(From 2 Kings 2:11, where the Old Testament prophet Elijah is taken directly to heaven: 'And it came to pass, as they still went on, and talked, that behold, there appeared a chariot of fire, and horses of fire, and parted them both asunder; and Elijah went up by a whirlwind into heaven.')

I will not cease from mental fight

(A non-violent struggle to cleanse the nation)

Not shall my Sword sleep in my hand

(Used metaphorically to denote the strength and will to fight against the dark)

Till we have built Jerusalem

In England's green and pleasant land.

'Jerusalem' was first performed at the Royal Albert Hall in 1916 by the Royal Choral Society, and has been sung there more times than any other song apart from the national anthem.

'LAND OF HOPE AND GLORY'

The music was written by Edward Elgar, forming part of the Trio section in his *Pomp and Circumstance March No. 1*, which received its successful premiere in Liverpool on 19 October 1901, with the composer conducting. Just three days later, the work had a triumphant reception at its first Proms appearance at the Queen's Hall.

It was King Edward VII who told Elgar he thought the melody would make a great song. When Elgar was requested to write a work for the king's coronation in 1902, the poet and essayist A.C. Benson helped him to create the *Coronation Ode*, which included the Trio's tune in its climax, with lyrics by Benson.

It was played as 'Land of Hope and Glory' as the opening number at the Last Night of the Proms in 1905. In subsequent years, Elgar's *Pomp and Circumstance March*

No. 1 became a regular fixture at the Last Night, with the audience joining in for the words of the tune to 'Land of Hope and Glory'.

Take a deep breath, and here we go (taking time to read the meanings behind the words, of course).

> Land of Hope and Glory,
> Mother of the Free,
> How shall we extol thee,
> Who are born of thee?
> (How can we who are born in Britain find words to express sufficient praise of the country?)
> Wider still and wider
> Shall thy bounds be set;
> (Encouraging a wider empire)
> God, who made thee mighty,
> Make thee mightier yet.
> God, who made thee mighty,
> Make thee mightier yet.

FUN FACT

BBC Proms presenter Katie Derham lives in the same house in Sussex where A.C. Benson once lived. He was also a master of Magdalene College, Cambridge, where she read economics.

THE NATIONAL ANTHEM

The origins of the British national anthem, the penultimate song at the Last Night, are hazy. There is no definitive writer or even definitive version of the lyrics.

The best claim to a 'standard' version was one close to the one we know today, published in 1745 in the *Gentleman's Magazine*. In September of that year, the 'Young Pretender' to the British throne, Charles Edward Stuart, defeated the army of King George II at Prestonpans, near Edinburgh. In a patriotic fervour, the leader of the band at the Theatre Royal, Drury Lane, arranged for three leading singers to sing 'God Save the King' after that night's performance of Ben Jonson's comedy, *The Alchemist*. It began: 'God bless our Noble King, God Save great George our King.' It was a tremendous success and was repeated nightly.

This practice soon spread to other theatres, and the custom of greeting monarchs with the song as he or she entered a place of public entertainment was established.

'For me, the locking of arms at the end singing "Auld Lang Syne" is always a very emotional moment. It feels really honest and genuine and so heartfelt. I find all of the patriotic songs quite emotional, really. There is rarely a moment in life where everybody is there to have a good time, where they are pre-disposed to have a great experience. I found that really thrilling'

– Marin Alsop, conductor

'AULD LANG SYNE'

The final parting of the ways before everyone goes home at the end of the Last Night is when Prommers and orchestra link arms for an informal rendition of 'Auld Lang Syne'. This is not part of the official proceedings, but a custom that began in the mid-1970s and has stuck ever since.

The title can be translated into English as 'old long since'. The Scottish bard, Robert Burns, did not create it, as he himself said. Rather he used an old folk song that had borrowed from other old folk songs and added verses to it.

Burns wrote down the words of the folk song after hearing an old man singing it, and in 1788 he sent a copy of it to his friend, Mrs Agnes Dunlop, saying, 'There is more of the fire of native genius in it than in half a dozen of modern English Bacchanalians!' Five years later he sent it to James Johnson, who was compiling a book of old Scottish songs called *Scots Musical Museum*. Burns said in his letter: 'The following song, an old song, of the olden times, and which has never been in print, nor even in manuscript until I took it down from an old man.'

The poem 'Old Long Syne', written by Robert Ayton and published in 1711 by James Watson, is often cited as Burns's inspiration. The Scottish poet Allan Ramsay published a poem in 1720 that began, 'Should auld acquaintance be forgot' but thereafter it was entirely different to the one that Burns wrote down.

There is no definitive source for the melody. English composer William Shield used a similar tune in his comic opera *Rosina*, first performed in 1781. It was not until 1799 that the familiar tune we know today was added to the words, three years after Burns's death.

The song reflects on old times with a childhood friend, encouraging them to have a goodwill drink together and shake hands for old time's sake.

Burns's original Scots verse:

Should auld acquaintance be forgot, and never brought to mind? Should auld acquaintance be forgot, and auld lang syne?

CHORUS: For auld lang syne, my jo, for auld lang syne, we'll tak' a cup o' kindness yet, for auld lang syne.

And surely ye'll be your pint-stoup! and surely I'll be mine!

And we'll tak' a cup o' kindness yet, for auld lang syne.
CHORUS

We twa hae run about the braes, and pou'd the gowans fine; But we've wander'd mony a weary fit, sin' auld lang syne.
CHORUS

We twa hae paidl'd in the burn, frae morning sun till dine; But seas between us braid hae roar'd sin' auld lang syne.

CHORUS

And there's a hand, my trusty fiere! and gie's a hand o' thine! And we'll tak' a right gude-willie waught, for auld lang syne.

CHORUS

The familiar English translation:

Should old acquaintance be forgot, and never brought to mind? Should old acquaintance be forgot, and auld lang syne?

CHORUS: For auld lang syne, my dear, for auld lang syne, we'll take a cup of kindness yet, for auld lang syne.

And surely you'll buy your pint cup! and surely I'll buy mine! And we'll take a cup o' kindness yet, for auld lang syne.

CHORUS

We two have run about the slopes, and picked the daisies fine; But we've wandered many a weary foot, since auld lang syne.

CHORUS

We two have paddled in the stream, from morning sun till down; But seas between us broad have roared since auld lang syne.

CHORUS

And there's a hand my trusty friend! And give me a hand o' thine! And we'll take a right good-will draught, for auld lang syne.

LOVING TRADITION

Mess with the Last Night at your peril. Prommers love the tradition and that means they don't appreciate change!

In 1969 the BBC decided to drop the performances of 'Land of Hope and Glory' and 'Rule, Britannia!' to make the event more attractive to viewers in Europe. But the decision was quickly overturned following public pressure.

Both songs were omitted in 2001, however, because the Last Night was the weekend after 9/11 and they were considered to be too high-spirited and not in touch with the sombre mood of the time. And the conductor was the American, Leonard Slatkin. The American national anthem was played, as well as the British. The evening ended with 'Jerusalem'.

The following year there was a compromise, of sorts, when Leonard Slatkin decided to play an instrumental version of 'Rule, Britannia!' without the soloist who traditionally leads Prommers through the seven verses whilst they enthusiastically join in with the chorus.

Slatkin explained that they were reflecting public opinion, telling the *Radio Times*,

'We have had a lot of letters saying that it is time to get rid of "Rule, Britannia!", and I must admit I am not completely comfortable with playing it. "Rule, Britannia!" does seem a little militaristic, and though it's wonderful to celebrate who you are and have faith in your country, I don't think we should exclude others. The Last Night of the Proms is an important occasion; in Japan they get up at 4am to watch it. Anyway, I'm not certain the sentiments of the words resonate in the way some people think they should. It does seem a little outdated.'

But there were many more letters complaining about the decision and the following year it was back in its usual traditional form.

In 2008 there was some shuffling of the traditional programme in which *Pomp and Circumstance March No. 1* was moved to after the conductor's speech and, shock of shocks, most of Wood's *Fantasia on British Sea-Songs* was replaced by Vaughan Williams's *Sea-Songs* as a final tribute in his anniversary year. But 'Bugle Calls' remained, as did 'Rule, Britannia!'.

The following year again saw the absence of 'Fantasia'. This time it was replaced by specially commissioned fanfares and extracts from Handel's *Music for the Royal Fireworks*.

RENEWING AND REFRESHING

Current Director of the BBC Proms, David Pickard, says he sees no reason to drop the Last Night favourites, but he does feel that they can be 'renewed and refreshed' ...

'I don't particularly want to mess with them in the sense that I don't think that I have any desire to drop them but, as so often, it's about renewing and refreshing things. I was talking the other day about the national anthem, for instance. It is a part of the Last Night and will always be there, but maybe in the future we will be thinking about getting some new people to arrange it so that we don't always hear the same version.

'"Rule, Britannia!", which is part of the Proms, has been sung by so many different singers and depending on whether it's a tenor or a baritone or bass or a soprano, it can be reinvented each year. So I think that the key to it is to keep the traditional moments but to find ways of touching them up a bit and blowing the dust off and make them feel a bit different.'

A CONSTANT DOUBLE ACT

Constance Shacklock sang at the Last Night a record-breaking ten times during the 1950s and 60s. Sarah Walker, who took over singing duties in 1985 and 1989, remembers her well:

'I used to watch the Last Nights of the Proms all the time with my parents when I was growing up. I remember the soloist always seemed to be Constance Shacklock, with Flash Harry, as he was called [Malcolm Sargent], conducting. I never had any special foreshadowing that one day I would be a part of it.'

GREAT LIVES

They are famous names, but here are a few things that you might not know about favourite composers that regularly feature at the Proms ...

EDWARD ELGAR

(b. 2 June 1857, d. 23 February 1934)

♪ His father had a music shop and tuned pianos in Worcester.

♪ In 1931, Elgar conducted 'Land of Hope and Glory' at the opening ceremony of Abbey Road Studios, which later became famous as the studio where The Beatles recorded.

♪ Each of the 14 variations in his *Enigma Variations* was related to a particular person in Elgar's life, and they were named after their initials or nicknames. For example, Variation 1 was inspired by his wife, Alice, and was named C.A.E. after her full name, Caroline Alice Elgar.

♪ Elgar enjoyed football and supported Wolverhampton Wanderers.

♪ He was a keen amateur chemist, happily spending hours in his shed on experiments. He invented the snappily titled Elgar Sulphuretted Hydrogen Apparatus, a device for synthesising hydrogen sulphide, and it briefly went into production.

CHARLES HUBERT PARRY

(b. 27 February 1848, d. 7 October 1918)

♪ Prince Charles is a fan of his works and feels he has been a neglected figure among the great composers.

♪ Four pieces by Parry were performed at the wedding ceremony of Prince William and Kate Middleton at

Westminster Abbey in 2011 – 'I Was Glad', 'Blest Pair of Sirens', 'March from the Birds' and 'Jerusalem'.

♪ His father and the parents of his bride-to-be, Elizabeth Maude Herbert, discouraged him from following a career in music, so instead he became an underwriter at Lloyd's of London, composing in his spare time.

♪ Parry was a huge admirer of German music and enjoyed German culture in general. He felt sure that Britain and Germany would never go to war against each other, and was in despair when the First World War broke out.

♪ 'Jerusalem' was adopted as the anthem of the Women's Institute.

THOMAS ARNE

(b. 12 March 1710, d. 5 March 1778)

♪ He was the leading figure in English theatrical music of his day.

♪ His grandfather fell on hard times and died in the debtors' prison of Marshalsea in Southwark, south London.

♪ Arne was so keen on music that he smuggled a spinet into his room and, damping the sounds with his handkerchief, would secretly practise during the night whilst the rest of the family slept.

♪ In 1732 he formed a small company with a group of friends that set out to perform opera solely in English.

♪ His 1762 opera *Artaxerxes* was an attempt – unique in musical history – to write an Italian tragic opera in English. It is about the prince of Persia who finds himself thrust into a position of power after the murders of his father and elder brother. It is regarded as one of Arne's masterpieces.

More Fascinating Facts on some of the most performed Last Night composers . . .

GIACOMO PUCCINI

(b. 22 December 1858, d. 29 November 1924)

♪ The premiere of his opera *Madama Butterfly* in 1904 at La Scala, Milan, was poorly received. But Puccini revised and restaged it, and it became a huge success.

♪ His three blockbuster operas, *Madama Butterfly*, *La Bohème* and *Tosca* made him very wealthy.

♪ His final opera *Turandot* was left incomplete at the time of his death from heart failure, but was completed from his sketches by fellow Italian composer Franco Alfano in time for its 1926 premiere.

♪ He loved his cars but was involved in a serious car accident in 1903, along with his wife Elvira and their son Antonio. A chauffeur was driving them to their home in Torre del Lago from Lucca when the car went off the road and flipped over. Elvira and Antonio were flung from the car and had minor injuries but Puccini was pinned under the vehicle before being rescued.

♪ Elvira publicly accused their young housemaid,

Doria Manfredi, of having an affair with her husband. Tragically she poisoned herself and her parents had her body examined by a physician, who declared her a virgin. They sued Elvira for slander, creating a huge scandal. Elvira was found guilty but escaped a prison sentence after Puccini paid damages to the Manfredi family.

RICHARD STRAUSS

(b. 11 June 1864, d. 8 September 1949)

- ♪ He used his considerable influence to prevent the Nazis from sending his Jewish daughter-in-law and grandchildren to concentration camps during the Second World War. He also refused to blacklist Jewish composers.

- ♪ His wife, the soprano Pauline de Ahna, was known to be eccentric and a diva.

- ♪ His father, Franz Joseph, was the principal horn player at the Munich Court Opera and he loathed the music of Richard Wagner. Young Richard was influenced by his father, sharing his dislike, but grew to admire Wagner.

- ♪ He preferred to write for the female voice and wrote some vocally taxing pieces, such as the frenzied finale of *Salome*.

- ♪ He was a keen player of a card game called skat. It helped him to relax. He explained that he could hear music everywhere and only the cards remained silent.

GIUSEPPE VERDI

(b. 10 October 1813, d. 27 January 1901)

♪ He became the official paid organist at his local church at the age of 12.

♪ Whilst working on his second opera, *Un giorno di regno*, Verdi's wife Margherita died of encephalitis at the age of 26. The comic opera premiered a few months later and was a flop. He vowed to give up composing forever but was persuaded to write *Nabucco*. Its premiere in 1842 made Verdi a star.

♪ In the mid-1840s he fell in love with soprano Giueseppina Strepponi, who was to become his lifelong companion. Their cohabitation before marriage was scandalous at the time.

♪ The great Italian composer's birth certificate is written in French because he was born in Le Roncole, a small town near Busseto, which was at that time under Napoleonic rule.

♪ An early passport for Verdi unflatteringly describes his appearance under 'special peculiarities' as 'pockmarked'!

CHAPTER 6

PROMENADERS AND PRANKS

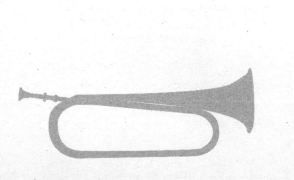

'I love being so close to the Promenaders
in the arena and I love their exuberance
and their enthusiasm. I thought it was
fantastic. It was such a great experience.

'The more going on, the happier I am.
I thrive on chaos! It's fun, and it's great to
be part of such an enthusiastic evening
and such a wonderful celebration. It starts
from even before the concert begins.
Walking up the hill and everybody
wanting your picture and autograph
and a chat, it just feels like they
can't wait.

'It's rare that you go to do a concert where
everybody is there because they really
want to be'

– Marin Alsop, conductor

The Promenaders in the arena, snuggling close to the
orchestra, are very much a part of the Last Night entertainment. Many of them are familiar faces and, like seasoned
entertainers, they know what is expected of them and how
to deliver it.

When it comes to making the most of the occasion, there are certain traditions to be followed. This often involves those in the arena doing a 'double act' with their gallery colleagues, as well as making the right moves for the 'Fantasia' section. So, if you're a Last Night novice, follow this simple guide to becoming a proper Prommer.

'A' REMARKABLE PERFORMANCE

Whilst the orchestra is settling in prior to accompanying a pianist, the latter will play an A for the players to tune their instruments to. As soon as you hear it, applaud like mad as if it is the finest piece of music you have heard all season!

GIVING THE 'HEAVE! HO!'

When the grand piano is wheeled to the front of the stage, if you are in the arena, shout 'Heave!' as the lid is being lifted. If you are in the gallery, this is your cue to respond with 'Ho!'

MULTILINGUAL

Visiting orchestras should be welcomed in their own language, if possible, or in an appropriate accent for English-speaking countries. For example, the Australian Youth Orchestra was greeted with a cheery 'G'day. Welcome to the pommie Proms.' Kiri Te Kanawa, who is from New Zealand, was greeted in Maori.

'CUTTING' REMARK

Another traditional favourite is this shout from below to above, which never fails to raise a laugh: 'Arena to gallery: short back and sides, not much on top, and something for the weekend, please.'

WHAT A RACQUET!

A favourite way to pass the time before the concert begins is with a spot of verbal to-ing and fro-ing. From the arena comes the invite, 'Anyone for tennis?' Then it's game on. There will be a loud 'ping' as the ball is 'served' from the arena and a 'pong' as it is returned from the gallery. This can go on for some time!

QUITE A FEET

A handy tip is to let your feet do the applauding for an exceptional performance. Someone will start to stamp their feet slowly and the others then join in, gradually picking up speed until it all gets out of hand – or foot!

ANCHORS AWEIGH

The *Fantasia on British Sea-Songs* is when Promenaders, who have gradually been gearing up throughout the evening, really let fly. Flags, balloons, floating inflated parrots, party poppers, rattles, whistles, squeaky ducks etc. are to the fore.

Here's what to do and when ...

'BUGLE CALLS'

Proud and slow flag waving accompanies the opening call to arms played on bugles.

'THE SAUCY ARETHUSA'

The jaunty opening notes on the euphonium representing daily life and high spirits at sea is the cue for crackers to go off in the audience and for mass bobbing up and down like corks on the water.

'TOM BOWLING'

A complete change of mood as we turn to the most mournful instrument in the orchestra, the cello, to signify the death aboard ship of British sailor, Tom Bowling. This produces perhaps the most bizarre ritual among Prommers of mass crying and the reaching for their handkerchiefs to wipe away their tears!

On one occasion, a clothes line of attached handkerchiefs was passed along the front row of the arena so that several people could attempt to curtail their grief at the same time!

'JACK'S THE LAD (HORNPIPE)'

Now the crew of the *Arethusa* need cheering up, so the jaunty sailor's hornpipe comes into play.

Although hornpipes were traditionally danced in bare feet, the Prommers keep their shoes on and bob up and down once more, clapping to the infectious notes of the violins, solo flute and solo piccolo, with many members of the audience hooting their horns in what they judge to be the right places! As the music gets faster and faster, so does the clapping and bobbing, and it's a race to the end. A huge cheer comes after the crescendo, followed by hearty applause. But there's little time to catch breath as a quick reprise is faster still.

The leader of the orchestra who plays the solo horn-pipe at the beginning of the piece sometimes plays a few tricks on the audience. There may be a surprise note or two, and when Stephen Bryant, a hornpipe veteran, was playing in 2017 he slipped in a few bars from the James Bond theme. This was greeted with much laughter.

'HOME, SWEET HOME'

Now we head homewards after the battle at sea. A solo clarinet then goes into a familiar refrain, accompanied by mass humming and swaying from the audience.

'SEE, THE CONQU'RING HERO COMES'

The celebration of victory, played on trumpets followed by French horns, has Prommers merrily whistling along.

TIMING IS ALL

Conductor Sir Andrew Davis hated the sound of popping balloons at the Last Night.

'The balloon thing used to drive me crazy. It wasn't people deliberately bursting them with a pin. It's hot in the hall and they would go off spontaneously. But yet I remember being distinctly infuriated because a balloon burst during a very beautiful cello solo in the "Tom Bowling" bit of Henry Wood's "Sea-Songs". I just had to grit my teeth and carry on.'

A CHUCKLE WITH HENRY

Representatives of the Prommers who adorn Sir Henry Wood's bust with a laurel chaplet often wipe an imaginary bead of sweat from his forehead, to the amusement of the crowd.

WAVING THE FLAG

It's strange to think now, when watching the swirl of hundreds of flags swaying to the music in the Royal Albert Hall, that nobody waved flags before 1947. It was only when the Last Night was shown on television that audiences, buoyed by patriotism and pride after the Second World War, started to bring and wave flags, enjoying the spectacle of it all.

However, flags played a part in the Proms even when the Queen's Hall was home. During the First World War they were hung over the organ to represent the countries of the Allies. By 1918 there were eight such flags.

FLAG UP

If you are going to wave the Union flag then it's useful to know something about its history ...

♪ The Union flag, or Union Jack, is the national flag of the United Kingdom.

♪ It dates back to 1606 when James I of Scotland, who had ascended to the English throne three years earlier, gave orders for a British flag to be created that bore the combined crosses of St George and of St Andrew. The red cross on white of St George, patron saint of England, was joined by the diagonal white cross on blue of St Andrew, patron saint of Scotland.

♪ The Welsh dragon does not appear on the Union flag because Wales was already united with England by this time and was no longer a separate principality. Its place in the flag is represented by the cross of Saint George.

♪ In 1707 the Acts of Union were passed, leading to the creation of the United Kingdom.

♪ The term Union Jack was traditionally used for the flag flown from Royal Navy ships, although the Flag Institute says the names Union flag or Union Jack can be used both at sea and ashore.

♪ The origin of the word 'Jack' is uncertain. It may refer to the shortening of the Latin version of James, 'Jacobus', or derive from a proclamation by Charles II that the Union flag should be flown only by ships of the Royal Navy as a 'jack', a small flag at the bowsprit. The term 'jack' once meant small.

♪ The Acts of Union with Ireland in 1800 led to the red diagonal cross of their patron saint, St Patrick, being added to the Union Flag. This is the flag we know today.

♪ The Union flag survived the partition of Ireland in 1921 and the St Patrick element of it continues to represent the place of Northern Ireland within the United Kingdom.

♪ It should always be flown the right way up. In the half of the flag nearest the flagpole, the wider diagonal white stripe must be above the red diagonal stripe.

♪ The flag is twice as wide as it is high.

DUCKING OUT

The removal of the Proms fountain from the middle of the Royal Albert Hall arena in 2011 caused an outcry, with over 1,000 Prommers signing a petition for it to be replaced. The small pool with fountain and water plants had been present since 1927 when the BBC took over the running of the Proms, but it was removed to increase capacity.

The fountain was originally designed to regulate the temperature of the Queen's Hall. At the RAH, the seating encircling it provided a welcome resting place, particularly for the elderly. Promenaders also enjoyed the fun of floating rubber ducks on it and other inflatable sea life. Roger Wright, director of the Proms and controller of Radio 3 in 2011, wrote in his blog: 'Promenaders will no doubt miss the chance to float an often surreal mix of inflatable creatures on the circular pond!'

'Once you are on that stage the Promenaders make you feel totally relaxed and you know that you have, most probably, the best musical audience in front of you, wanting to enjoy the evening as much as you want to. So it's a kind of team effort between the orchestra, the choir, the soloists, the performers, the audience, even the Royal Albert Hall itself. The Last Night of the Proms is a wonderful denouement to the weeks and months of preparation and hard work and dedication'

– Bryn Terfel, singer

TUT-TUT!

Not everyone enjoys the Promenaders' high spirits. They have often been criticised for crossing the line in their behaviour. Henry Wood's partner, Jessie, made her displeasure felt after the Last Night of 1948 when the audience was whipped up to a frenzy by Sargent after 'Land of Hope and Glory' and 'Fantasia'. After Sargent thanked everyone and announced a series of winter concerts, there followed what one journalist described as 'an almost hysterical outburst from the packed crowd'. But Jessie Wood complained that the 'audience was there more for a good time than for self-improvement'.

A journalist from *The Times* went even further by saying that 'hooliganism was rather too evident. High-spirited gratitude must not be confused with sheer bad manners.'

Stanford Robinson, who had conducted the Last Night the previous year, agreed. 'The good humour of previous generation of Prom-goers seems to have degenerated into hooliganism to a marked degree.' Robinson suggested scrapping the 'Sea-Songs' in future, whilst fellow Last Night Conductor, Basil Cameron, proposed just omitting the hornpipe.

The eventual decision was to replace Sargent as Last Night conductor for a more restraining hand in the shape of Adrian Boult. But he was the wrong man for the job. He looked uncomfortable and did nothing to restore order, despite 'Land of Hope and Glory' being dropped. The following year, Sargent was back. And excited Prom-enaders got even more exuberant when 'Land of Hope and Glory' returned. BBC Controller of the Light Programme, Tom Chalmers, described the experience as a 'frightening emotional orgy!'

Both Sargent and Basil Cameron shared the Last Night conducting in 1952, before Sargent went it alone the following year, with the finale featuring 'Land of Hope and Glory', Arne's 'Rule, Britannia!' and Parry's 'Jerusalem'. There was no 'Sea-Songs'. By 1954 the template was in place. There was no going back!

FOLLOWING FLASH HARRY

'I always used to approach the Last Night with a mixture of eager anticipation and dread,' conductor Sir Andrew Davis says. 'Because it was such fun and a wonderful celebration at the end of the season and people are there because they love the music but they also love a good time, and so the spirit was always extraordinarily upbeat and fun but sometimes the dread part was, "Will I be able to control this lot?"

'But it's interesting, this whole relationship with the Promenaders at the Last Night. I suppose I took my cue from Malcolm Sargent, who was the ultimate showman when he conducted the Last Night. 'Flash Harry' was his nickname. He had this great badinage with the Promenaders and would quietly abuse them and get away with it! So I took a leaf out of his book in saying what a terrible lot they were! And that became part of the Last Night tradition, as it had been with Sargent.'

LOSING CONTROL

On one occasion, Sir Andrew Davis's own exuberance backfired somewhat when he made Promenaders over-excited before the second half 'party' had even begun.

'In the first half there tend to be some quite serious pieces. But I do remember one year [1994] we did *Belshazzar's Feast* by William Walton in the first half, and it was one of the fastest performances ever and the audience went crazy! They got themselves so wound up that when we came to the second half they were sort of uncontrollable!

'When it came to making the speech there was a lot of heckling, but in a fun way, of course. I remember Sir John Drummond [Director of the BBC Proms] and me thinking, "Well, what are we going to do next year so we don't have the same problem?"

'As it happened, the following year featured the premiere of Harrison Birtwistle's 1995 strident, contemporary piece, *Panic*, in the second half, which left those desperately waiting for the traditional favourites rather bemused. This was not a typical lead-in by any means.

'The following year it was back to the classics with the Prelude and the "Liebestod" from *Tristan and Isolde* by Wagner. A rather sombre piece carefully chosen to please yet not over-excite!'

THANK YOU GIFTS

Over the years it had become a tradition for the Prommers to present the conductor and soloists with a gift at the end of the Last Night. Helen Heslop, BBC Live Events team manager, explains how the gift-giving works:

'A group of Prommers ask me in August who they are giving gifts to this year and then they buy them. They could be anything from beautiful paper-weights to a bottle of something special but it's usually something Proms-related or that they have had made specially.

'The Prommers who are presenting the gift come in the afternoon to do a little rehearsal, where we bring them backstage and walk them through. To them it's a mammoth deal because they are on show, so we reassure them and get them to walk their route and try it out with their presents in their hands and then I'll cue them on the night itself to say, "Right, go now." It doesn't always go smoothly though. One or two have gone wrong in the past because we didn't cue them quickly enough and the conductor came off before they could hand over the present. We have learnt over the years to send them straight out, to avoid disappointment.'

'The last gift I got from the Prommers was very nice. It was a silver hip flask covered in leather, and it's a beautiful thing. And, I have to confess, I have used it a couple of times!'

— Sakari Oramo, Chief Conductor, BBC Symphony Orchestra

A TIGHTS SPOT

Conductor Vernon Handley got a big laugh after the Promenaders brought up their traditional gifts for the conductor and singer of 'Rule, Britannia!', Sarah Walker, in 1985. They both opened their presents and she took out a pen. When Handley opened his, he joked, 'Tights?' He looked genuinely startled when he actually saw what he had been given – the face of an owl on a plaque.

SMART GIVING

In addition to presenting gifts to these key performers, the Prommers make up buttonholes for all the musicians on stage – typically numbering more than 250 with orchestra, choirs and soloists combined. It's a tradition that began soon after the death in 1967 of Last Night favourite Malcolm Sargent, whose carnation buttonhole was a noted feature of his immaculate podium presentation. The gifts and buttonholes are paid for from a collection taken along the Promming queues during the season.

Another even more altruistic tradition arose around the first Prommers' collection. The money left over after covering the costs of gifts and carnations was donated to the charity Malcolm Sargent Cancer Care for Children. Nearly 50 years later, Prommers now shake their yellow buckets at the Royal Albert Hall exits after each prom, encouraging the entire audience (not just Prommers) to donate to musical charities. In 2017 the total raised was over £115,000.

PROMENADER PARTICIPATION

'It's always a very nice moment when the Promenaders come and do something,' says conductor Sir Andrew Davis. 'Laying the wreath on Sir Henry's bust is a moment to show that they are not just there to cause a ruckus! They are there to remember the founder and to show their gratitude for what he has done and everyone involved has done, and giving a little gift to the conductor is a very nice gesture as well.'

PREPARE TO PROM

GETTING A TICKET

The majority of tickets for the Last Night of the Proms are allocated by ballot to customers who have bought tickets to at least five other Proms concerts at the Royal Albert Hall and another 200 tickets are allocated by the Open Ballot. A maximum of two tickets for the Last Night is allowed per application.

A very small number of tickets can be purchased at the Royal Albert Hall by turning up on the Last Night itself and no previous ticket purchases are necessary. But you'd have to be quick to get them!

Helen Heslop, BBC Live Events team manager, has this tip for anyone wanting to attend the Last Night ...

'You can just simply turn up and queue to get into the arena and I don't think we have ever turned anyone away, but people don't tend to come and queue for Last Night because they assume they won't get in. So, if you are asking me, I would say, get there early, queue up and come in.'

Hardcore Promenaders are all season-ticket holders. These tickets guarantee admission to the Last Night. Information on getting tickets can be found in the Festival Guide and on the Royal Albert Hall website.

WHERE TO STAND

Arena or gallery?
Prommers have the choice of either standing in the arena or the gallery – the promenade areas.

The arena
Those who stand here are the life and soul of the Proms – the loudest, most enthusiastic members of the audience. Their closeness to the orchestra and conductor builds a rapport with the performers.

'The arena is the best place to be if you don't mind standing. You get the best sound in the arena'

– Helen Heslop, BBC Live Events team manager

The gallery

Standing right at the very top of the Albert Hall provides a unique view of the Proms in its full splendour. Some prefer this and vouch for the feeling of camaraderie here. The stage may seem a long way away but the sound is surprisingly good. There is also more space to 'promenade' – walk around a bit – in the traditional fashion.

GET IN LINE

Queuing to get in is a long-held tradition to ensure that you get your favoured position. This can start in the early hours of the morning, or even overnight, or longer for the faithful. This may seem like a chore, but most Prommers feel it is very much part of the event and enjoy the sense of camaraderie that ensues. Folding chairs, books, playing cards, flasks etc., are part of the recommended equipment. Once your position has been established it is deemed acceptable to briefly leave the queue to eat, buy a cup of tea or go to the toilet before resuming your place, but plonking down your belongings and then disappearing for hours used to be seen as a definite no-no. But this tradition changed somewhat when, in 2017, for the first time, a queue-numbering system was introduced so that there was no need to queue all day or camp overnight.

Those with tickets and even hopefuls yet to get one were able to request a queue number from a steward outside Door 12 at 12–10pm on the day before the Last Night and again from 9am on the day itself. Once they had their numbers they had to return to the queue by

5.30pm on the day of the concert to claim their spot. The queue number dictated the point at which you would be permitted to enter the Hall. Stewards were on hand to supervise.

EXCUSE ME!

Richard Baker, who presented the Proms for the BBC for many years, admitted that his father found a 'short cut' to getting his hands on a couple of Last Night tickets ...

'My father was a plasterer by trade and had very little money, but he was a passionate music lover and the Proms provided such people with a wonderful opportunity to get to know the repertoire. I was 11 in 1936 and he decided that we would go to the Last Night of the Proms. We didn't have any tickets and what he did was to barge into the queue – he didn't mind cheating a bit!'

PRIME POSITIONS

The front row of the arena, next to the rail, which can accommodate about 25 people, is the prime site. But be warned, there are devoted Promenaders who come back year after year and expect to take up their 'rightful' positions!

WEAR WITH FLAIR

There is no formal dress code. Some Prommers like to go the full 'Brit bit' in Union flag-emblazoned clothes or wear dinner jackets or elegant gowns. Others prefer to be comfortable in T-shirts or other casual wear. Accessories include flags of many nations, balloons, party poppers and duck whistles.

BBC PROMS FESTIVAL GUIDE

Get a copy of this to help you to plan your summer of music and discover in depth what lies behind the Proms – from the composers to the performers to how the events are broadcast. Check the BBC Proms website for how to pre-order a copy in print or as an eBook. It is also available in bookshops.

'Ticket prices are not a hindrance for anyone to attend these concerts, and the sheer range of music that is played throughout every Proms season is more than anywhere else in the world'

– Sakari Oramo, Chief Conductor, BBC Symphony Orchestra

CHAPTER 7

LIGHTS, CAMERA, ACTION!

'The Proms are a really important British export, particularly the Last Night. Of course, we can see it as patriotic but with the Last Night we can send messages around the world and make sure it is something that people see as a really important part of what Britain has to offer in terms of culture'

– Sakari Oramo, Chief Conductor, BBC Symphony Orchestra

Broadcasting to millions around the world, the Last Night of the Proms is a mammoth undertaking involving cameras, microphones, lights, a well-drilled team each knowing exactly what they are responsible for and, crucially, minute-by-minute timing. Here we meet some of those responsible for spreading the spectacle around the world and learn how it has evolved into the major broadcasting event that it is today.

A TRADITIONAL APPEAL

The second half of the Last Night certainly has a patriotic if not a jingoistic tone, yet it is loved around the world.

BBC Proms Director David Pickard has pondered this peculiarity himself. And he's come up with this answer …

'I often ask myself why the Last Night is so popular around the world. I think, in a way, there is something about that British tradition that is very appealing to a foreign audience. The clichéd Englishman with the bowler hat is something that people around the world have a great love and affection for.

'One of the nicest things on the Last Night of the Proms is that it does really feel like an international occasion. Yes, there's a very British feel to the music that we play, but when I walk down the Proms queue – and that's what I did in my first Proms – the first flag that I saw was Japanese and the second one was German, and it was a long while before I got to a Union Jack. The Last Night is celebrated as much as an international festival as it is a British one.'

THE FIRST BROADCASTS

When the Proms were first broadcast from the Queen's Hall on 13 August 1927, there was an initial nervousness among those involved. Some felt that broadcasting the BBC Proms would result in people staying away from attending the event itself. Twenty years after that first broadcast, and still playing to a packed auditorium, it was to become a television event. The first prom to be televised was the Last

Night on 13 September 1947, from the Royal Albert Hall. Just two cameras were used.

The great showman, Malcolm Sargent, had become chief conductor in 1947 and at the Last Night he conducted the first half of the proceedings in which Mendelssohn's Piano Concerto No. 1 was performed, along with 'Mars' and 'Jupiter' from Holst's *The Planets*. His showmanship stood out and he flourished in the spotlight under the gaze of the cameras. The second half was conducted by Basil Cameron, concluding with Wood's *Fantasia on British Sea-Songs*.

But the Proms would not make it back onto television again until 1953, when Sargent dominated the broadcast of the First and Last Nights.

David Pickard, Director of the BBC Proms, explains that many were highly wary of television in this period:

'I know some of my predecessors were nervous about television, and there's always been a worry, from the very early days, that if you broadcast a concert then nobody will want to come and see it live. And it's clearly not the case because the fact that we play to 89 per cent capacity houses every year, despite having 25 live Proms on television and all of them live on Radio 3, shows that there is an audience that see it live as well as one that watches it on television.'

After 1953 it became an annual television event, with Sargent at the forefront of turning the Last Night from what had been, until then, a relatively sober occasion into a joyous celebration in which he encouraged the audience to play as much a part as the performers. The visual element was all, and Promenaders increasingly brought with them flags, horns and balloons as their outfits became more and more colourful.

The Director of the BBC Proms at the time, William Glock, did his best to subdue the fervent, patriotic tone of the Last Night but Sargent was in his element, particularly in his banter with his beloved Promenaders.

'I like these interruptions,' he said at one point to those gathered in the arena. 'It gives me time to think of the next sentence.' And when a balloon burst he assured listeners on the radio that he had not been assassinated.

BROADCASTING MILESTONES

♪ 1927: The Proms are first broadcast on radio.

♪ 1947: The Last Night is the first Prom to be televised.

♪ 1970: The Proms are televised in colour.

♪ 1989: High definition brings clarity to the Proms.

♪ 2016: Binaural sound is introduced at some of the concerts, providing an immersive experience mimicking the shape of the human head via special microphones in the rigging.

♪ 2017: Experiments with binaural sound continue with a mix of the Last Night favourites able to be heard on the internet by using headphones.

LET THERE BE LIGHT

Bernie Davis is Television Lighting Designer at the BBC Proms. Here he throws some light on what his job entails and how it has evolved over the years ...

How long have you been doing this job?

'I have been lucky enough to have lit the Proms since 1993, although my history with the Proms goes back even further to times when I was a Vision Engineer with BBC Outside Broadcasts.

'When I arrived at the Proms they were lit with a basic wash of light but I soon learnt that the lighting had to achieve more than to make television pictures – it had to satisfy the orchestras, the Royal Albert Hall, the Promenaders and even Radio 3. Television seemed relatively low on the priority list. The orchestra must have enough light to read the scores, no light in their eyes, and be able to see the conductor comfortably. The Royal Albert Hall want their venue to be presented at its best at this major event in their calendar. The Promenaders have paid – a small ticket price – to see a classical concert and Radio 3 wants lighting that is silent! With a little compromise that is what we deliver.

'Only a few concerts per year were televised at first, and the numbers slowly increased over the years. In 1993 we broadcast a total of 11. This number increased significantly with the introduction of the digital channels to around the 25 we now cover. This means I have lit more televised Proms than everyone else who has ever lit them put together!'

What does your job involve?

'My lighting is used on every prom in the Hall, but we grade them into categories before the season in order to be as economical as possible. If it is a straightforward orchestral concert, not taken by television, then just one person from my crew looks after the lighting. Sometimes a late-night prom might have slightly greater needs, but again one carefully chosen crew member is scheduled. If the concert is televised then I oversee it, and I have two crew members to deal with maintenance and to light any interviews and presenters.

'Then there are the complex Proms, from the *Dr Who* prom to staged operas, which might not be on television but still have big demands on lighting design and operation, and I oversee these together with as many crew as they demand.

'Some people question why special lighting is needed for a radio concert, but of course these are concerts for a live audience of up to 6,000 people, and these days people's expectations of lighting are higher than ever. You only have to look at the Radio 1 Ibiza prom to see how much the lighting can contribute to the atmosphere of the occasion.'

How has the lighting evolved over the years?

'The lighting rig changes a little every year, and the rules in 1993 were that only white light could be used for classical music. I did not agree and tried to slowly change things. As a lighting designer I am very aware of the enhancements that lighting can offer an event.

'The first year I lit the Proms we had about 70 lights over the stage and probably a similar number spread around the rest of the hall.

'Each of these had to be cabled to behind the organ at the top level of the hall where we install dimmers and control equipment. The average cabling distance would be about 80 metres, so you can see the amount of cable even then was significant.

'My stock answer when asked how much cable we now use is that it is enough to go around the world twice – but I won't specify at which latitude!

'Over the years the equipment has changed with the times, and one of the early driving forces was, of all things, *Blue Peter*. When a *Blue Peter* prom was first staged in the 1990s, the producer was keen to use coloured lighting and make more of a contemporary concert of it, designed to appeal to a younger audience. As this was a televised prom, we had the budget to get in some extra lighting.

'The TV production team noticed that the concert was enhanced by the use of colour and patterns, and they started to ask for this on their concerts too. This was the driving force to start lifting the original rule of "only white light" at the Proms.

'We now have a rig that can easily change style with colour-changing lights that can enhance not only the stage, but also the organ, the mushrooms on the ceiling and the arches in the gallery. We make a point of keeping most concerts looking classical, though, and save the more colourful looks for the right occasions.'

What does the lighting usually consist of today?

'In 2017 we used a total of around 390 conventional lights and about 200 intelligent lights – lights that can move or change colour – or both. Another part of the lighting rig introduced in 2010 is the LED display panel at the back of the stage. We were asked to make the television Proms look more up-to-date and this was a way of moving design into an area that would be seen on camera. We initially provided abstract graphics designed to complement the mood and style of the music, but once its value was appreciated it has contributed more and more to the look of the stage.'

How do you prepare it all?

'The first week of the Proms is taken up with rigging and preparing everything. Several truck-loads of lighting and cabling is delivered on the Monday morning, and by the evening the rig over the stage is rigged and cabled onto the RAH lighting trusses, and also onto additional trusses that we provide.

'By Tuesday lunchtime it has to be taken up to the height required for best acoustics, and from that point it cannot be lowered again for two months as all the microphone slings for radio and television are rigged below. From that point the only access to the lighting is by climbing a caving ladder made of steel wire, and then walking the truss 10 metres over the stage. The rest of Tuesday is spent rigging lighting in the gallery and on the circle front, and also setting up the lighting control to drive all the lighting. Wednesday is a focus day when every light is set in the right position for its purpose. On Thursday morning we finish rigging other areas such as the presenters' positions, and we also check the lighting balance over the stage to make sure it is ready for the orchestral rehearsal that afternoon.'

Do things change much over the season?

'Having made the main rig work at the start of the season, we hope to not change it for the whole season, and that is why we can work with such a small crew and within the limits of the demanding Proms schedule, which has at least one rehearsal and one concert per day, and often two of both.

'We only add equipment for special Proms where maybe lights on stage might add to the occasion – in particular the jazz concerts and occasions like the Quincy Jones Prom. We have lit music stands for these concerts too, enabling the musicians to read the music whilst we take the lighting down to a lower level over the stage.

'People are often surprised they aren't used on every concert, but musicians are not keen to use them if they can be avoided, and TV directors are often not happy as they can block shots of the musicians.'

Are there any particular changes to the lighting for the Last Night?

'As the rig is so flexible now, the Last Night of the Proms is really just another concert in the series for us, although we do add some extra audience lighting for the "Land of Hope and Glory" moment.'

What changes do you see for the future?

'Even after 25 years the rig updates a little each year, and next I want to try to introduce extra LED lighting to make the rig more energy-efficient. We already have many energy-efficient lighting units in the rig, but I really want to see if I can make the main orchestral lighting more eco-friendly. Every year the lighting moves on, just a little at a time.'

NOT TUNED IN

The Last Night of the Proms wasn't broadcast in Finland when Last Night conductor Sakari Oramo was growing up and so he only came to it later in life.

'It was not part of my upbringing and so I came to it fresh,' he says. 'Before I conducted my first Last Night I listened to the 2012 one on the radio conducted by Jiří Bělohlávek, mainly for the purpose of informing myself. Of course, it was not the same as watching on television because you don't see all the colours and activity.'

When he came to doing it for real in 2014, Oramo felt that he was quite well prepared:

'The days leading up to the Last Nights are always quite hectic and there is so much activity going on. There is much more music than is usual in such a time span and it's also small bits and pieces of music, which makes it harder to rehearse. And the presence of television is always a little bit disconcerting. There are lights and people running around more than usual. But I tend to think that it is always for the good of the art and therefore I get by.'

'The BBC does such a wonderful job of organising. They have got it down to a science and every second is accounted for, so you know exactly what is going on. I never felt there was anything that took me by real surprise. I was prepared for all of the traditions and I think they are lovely. That is something that appeals to me about Britain. I love having well-respected and centuries-old traditions. There is something really comforting about that'

— Marin Alsop, conductor

A TASTE OF BRITAIN

In Japan, people get up in their millions at four o'clock in the morning to watch the Last Night of the Proms on TV, enjoying the spectacle of such a British tradition. And in Germany 'British parties' are held in Berlin, where the concert is watched on television as they dine on bangers and mash!

'The biggest logistical challenge is trying to make sure that, given the sheer crazy schedule we have where there are often two concerts a day, we get everything to run smoothly so that when BBC Radio 3 goes live, the orchestra is ready to play. That involves such a well-drilled operation backstage, and we are so lucky that we have these amazing people – stage managers, technicians, orchestra managers – who somehow make all those things happen. On a typical day, you might have a total of two rehearsals and two concerts all happening between eight o'clock in the morning and midnight, so it really is an extraordinary operation'

– David Pickard, Director of the BBC Proms

CHAPTER 8

TAKING UP THE BATON

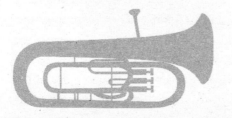

'The Proms is something very special and it's very British, and it gets idiotically British on the Last Night'

— Sir Andrew Davis, conductor

Being a conductor at the Proms is a prestigious position, but taking up the baton for the Last Night takes a special person with a love of fun and audience participation, combined with leadership and authority.

Since Sir Henry Wood conducted his last concert in 1944, many a distinguished name has led the orchestra at the climactic Proms concert but, for sheer flair and unashamed showmanship, one name will always be remembered.

MALCOLM SARGENT

LAST NIGHTS: 1947, 1948, 1950–1966

True to his keenness to encourage and promote youth and up-and-coming talent, on 11 October 1921 Henry Wood asked the little-known composer and conductor Malcolm Sargent to guest conduct his own composition *An Impression on a Windy Day* at that season's Last Night of the Proms concert in the Queen's Hall. He was just 26 years old. It was to lead to Sargent becoming the chief conductor of the Proms from 1947 until his death in

1967. He took part in 514 concerts, shaping it to the form we know today.

After that first concert, Sargent was invited back with his compositions a handful of times and Wood encouraged him as a conductor. In 1947, during his first season as chief conductor, Sargent conducted the first ever televised concert in Britain.

His reign coincided with a new, national feeling of relief and patriotism after the Second World War. Sargent's flair, showmanship and ability to naturally engage with the audience made him hugely popular with Promenaders and, later, with the millions watching on TV around the world. It was he who filled the Last Night with a sense of fun and celebration.

Sargent was noted for his immaculate appearance – he always wore evening dress with a carnation buttonhole – and his witty speeches.

On the eve of the 1967 Proms he was too ill to conduct and reluctantly stepped down. He conducted no other concerts but, ever the showman, he was determined to make an appearance at the Last Night. He made a short speech in which he praised the BBC SO and the 'new and very gifted conductor Colin Davis'. At the end, he said that he had one more thing to say: 'Next year the Promenade concerts begin on 20 July, and I have been invited to be here that night.' A huge cheer sounded. He added, 'I have accepted the invitation. God willing, we will all meet again then.' Again, there was a rousing cheer. He turned and left the podium. But it was to be his last appearance. Seventeen days later, on 3 October 1967, he died, at the age of 72.

THE MAKING OF A CONDUCTOR

Malcolm Sargent was born in Ashford, Kent, the son of working-class parents who happened to love music. His father was a coal merchant and part-time church organist. His mother was the matron of a local school.

The young Sargent was brought up in Stamford, Lincolnshire. A talented pianist and organist, he also conducted and produced the operas of Gilbert and Sullivan for the local operatic society. This got him noticed, most importantly, by Henry Wood.

'I think the Last Night is so popular around the world because of the incredibly celebratory and positive atmosphere on the night. Everyone has admiration and respect for the traditions of the UK. Also, I think that people appreciate the self-deprecating humour of the British people and that comes through. It's a celebration but it's also a little bit tongue in cheek. Plus there's a real sincerity and heart-on-your-sleeve quality about it that appeals to everyone'

— Marin Alsop, conductor

The full roll-call of the rest of the Last Night conductors to date ...

HENRY WOOD

1895–1938 & 1941–43

The inaugural Proms conductor, BBC SO chief conductor and BBC Director of Music Sir Henry Wood's reign was interrupted by the Second World War. The 1939 season opened but was curtailed by the outbreak of war. German bombing the following year meant there was no official Last Night. Wood resumed from 1941 onwards but the 1944 season was once more cut short due to renewed bombing. Wood died later that year.

ADRIAN BOULT

1945–47 & 1949

The new chief conductor of the BBC SO shared Last Night duties during the post-war period with Basil Cameron, Constant Lambert, Stanford Robinson and Malcolm Sargent.

Boult had been a director of the BBC SO from its founding in 1930. He was a striking figure, looking like a quintessential Englishman at six foot tall with a walrus moustache. Whilst his right hand flicked the baton crisply, his left hand barely moved. He disliked over-rehearsing a work, relying on his musicians and his experience.

BASIL CAMERON

1945, 1947–49 & 1952

At the start of the First World War, Basil Cameron's German immigrant parents discreetly dropped their Germanic surname of Hindenberg and the conductor used his middle name of Cameron as his professional surname. In 1940 he joined the conducting staff of the Proms as an associate conductor to Henry Wood. He had an unassuming manner and was popular with his orchestra and Prommers alike.

CONSTANT LAMBERT

1945

His intelligence, charm, wit and storytelling made him sparkling company. A talented composer and conductor, he had a louche air, enjoyed jazz and was founder Music Director of the Royal Ballet. He was staggeringly self-assured and confident.

STANFORD ROBINSON

1947

Robinson shared the Last Night podium with Boult, Sargent and Cameron. He studied at the Royal College of Music under Adrian Boult. From 1924 to 1966 he was on the staff of the BBC and went on to become the BBC's first chorus master. He established and developed the Wireless Chorus and Wireless Singers (now the BBC Singers), and the BBC National Chorus (now the BBC Symphony Chorus).

COLIN DAVIS

1967–72

Taking up the baton from Malcolm Sargent was never going to be an easy task and, at first, chief conductor Davis was overshadowed by the memory of Sargent at the Last Night. He raised eyebrows on the Last Night of 1968 when he abandoned a tailcoat for a white dinner jacket. Davis was less comfortable with the traditional high jinks but grew into the role and made his mark. He was well respected by his peers and audiences.

NORMAN DEL MAR

1973, 1975 & 1983

His energy was prodigious. A big man with big physical movements, he was known affectionately as 'the Mass of Life'.

Del Mar was the author of an acclaimed three-volume work on the life and music of Richard Strauss, and was Professor of Conducting at the Royal College of Music. He is remembered for his recordings of British music; in particular Elgar, Vaughan Williams, Delius and Britten.

CHARLES GROVES

1974, 1976 & 1978

Known for encouraging contemporary composers and young conductors, his enthusiasm for music meant he often went above and beyond the call of duty. For example, when the Bournemouth Municipal Orchestra, of which he was conductor, was in danger of disbanding during a financial crisis, he took to the streets to sell raffle tickets to raise money.

JAMES LOUGHRAN

1977, 1979, 1981–82 & 1984

Born in Glasgow, he became Music Director of the English Opera Group, chief conductor of the BBC Scottish Symphony Orchestra and conducted the first concert of the newly formed Scottish Chamber Orchestra in 1974. A popular figure at the Proms, he led the Last Night on five occasions.

CHARLES MACKERRAS

1980

He became the first non-Briton to conduct the BBC Symphony Orchestra at the Last Night of the Proms. Born in New York state, he was brought up in Sydney, Australia. His parents were keen on music but did not see it as a career and were reluctant to encourage their son. But his persistence led to them abandoning their plans for him to be a lawyer and they let him study music full-time.

VERNON HANDLEY

1985

As a schoolboy, he watched the BBC Symphony Orchestra playing at its studio in Maida Vale and learned some of his future conducting technique by observing Adrian Boult, who later took him on as his assistant. Through Boult he learned restraint – that the conductor's gestures were for the orchestra and not the audience. Handley's subsequent performances on the podium were even less obtrusive than his mentor's. But his orchestras loved him.

RAYMOND LEPPARD

1986

As well as conducting orchestras he composed several film scores, including *Lord of the Flies* (1963) and *Hotel New Hampshire* (1984), and his interest in baroque music helped to revive it in the 1960s.

MARK ELDER

1987 & 2006

After he questioned playing 'Land of Hope and Glory' and 'Rule, Britannia!' at the Last Night in 1990 during the time of the Gulf War, he was dismissed from that engagement. He returned in 2006 and during his conductor's speech he criticised aircraft baggage restrictions, which made it difficult for musicians to carry their instruments on board.

> 'Things don't often go wrong on the Last Night because it is so tightly run and there are endless meetings about it. So things usually go fine. Although conductor Mark Elder made a twenty-five-minute speech — that took us all by surprise!'
>
> **– Paul Hughes, General Manager of the BBC SO and Chorus, and the BBC Singers**

SIR ANDREW DAVIS

1988, 1990–92, 1994–2000 & 2018

Chief conductor Davis restored the tradition of fun and ebullient showmanship established by Malcolm Sargent. He was also noted for his humorous Last Night speeches. He became much loved by Prommers over the years and proved to be so popular that he chalked up 12 Last Nights.

'The Proms is one of the most extraordinary festivals of music. It's two months long and there is a concert every night, sometimes two concerts, and nowadays there are Proms going on outside the Albert Hall. There is a huge range of music and the whole festival is enormously varied and comprehensive, and then the Last Night is everyone letting their hair down until next year. It's a kind of party at the end of the festival. There's this spirit of enjoying the occasion, but not in a stuffy way'

– Sir Andrew Davis, conductor

SIR JOHN PRITCHARD

1989

He studied conducting under Sir Henry Wood, and later became chief conductor of the BBC Symphony Orchestra. Despite suffering from cancer, he fulfilled a lifelong desire to conduct the Last Night of the Proms in 1989, before dying just three months later.

'I sang on the Last Night of John Pritchard's final performance in the UK. He was a wonderful conductor and a lovely man.

He was so ill then that the big soloists' room that existed in the Albert Hall at the time was entirely given over to his medical team and he had an oxygen tent. We were all worried about him getting through the evening and thinking, "Just a bit further, John." At the end, the audience and orchestra stood and cheered. He leant on me and we started to walk off together, up through the orchestra,

and then halfway up he said, "Ah. I've forgotten something." I said, "Shall I get it for you?" and he said, "No, no. I'll get it." And he turned round, and on his own he walked back to the podium and picked up his present from the Promenaders, which was a bottle of whisky. He held it up to the audience and got another cheer as he walked off. And I'm afraid that we all knew that was the last we were going to see of him because

he was so ill. It's a bittersweet memory.
He was lovely'

– Sarah Walker, singer

BARRY WORDSWORTH

1993

He studied under Adrian Boult and Vernon Handley at the Royal College of Music. He became Music Director of the Royal Ballet Covent Garden and principal conductor of the BBC Concert Orchestra from 1989 to 2006. At the final concert held at the Adrian Boult Hall in Birmingham, Wordsworth was hero of the hour when he flew in from France to take the baton when the proposed conductor withdrew two days earlier.

LEONARD SLATKIN

2001–04

American Slatkin, who was chief conductor of the BBC SO, conducted his first Last Night in 2001, days after the 9/11 attacks. The atmosphere was more subdued than normal. The following year his desire to tone down the nationalism saw 'Rule, Britannia!' only heard as part of *Fantasia on British Sea-Songs*. This practice lasted until 2007. In 2003 he conducted a more traditional Last Night.

PAUL DANIEL

2005

Known for his droll sense of humour, he became Music Director of the English National Opera in 1997. As conductor of the Orchestre National Bordeaux Aquitaine, he illustrated how his well-drilled musicians did not require his services during a recital of Ravel's *Bolero*, when halfway through he took the top off a beer and strolled around drinking it, before raising it in toast to the amused audience!

JIŘÍ BĚLOHLÁVEK

2007, 2010 & 2012

The first non-native English speaker to conduct and make the traditional speech at the Last Night. The former Artistic Director of the Czech Philharmonic Orchestra and the founder of the Prague Philharmonia, he became chief conductor of the BBC SO in 2006. At the Last Night in 2009, he 'played' a vacuum cleaner in Malcolm Arnold's *A Grand, Grand Overture*.

ROGER NORRINGTON

2008

He liked to have fun with music and encouraged his musicians to enjoy themselves. In turn, they loved him. He disliked the stuffiness often associated with classical music, and he led the judging panel in the BBC TV entertainment show *Maestro* in 2008, in which eight celebrities with a passion for classical music competed for the chance to conduct the BBC Concert Orchestra at the 2008 Prom in the Park at Hyde Park.

DAVID ROBERTSON

2009

Born in Santa Monica, he moved to London at the age of 18 to study at the Royal Academy of Music. A champion of young musicians, he became Music Director of the St Louis Symphony Orchestra. Urbane and a natural communicator, during his Last Night speech he said that the 'wide diversity of instruments' in the orchestra are 'a powerful symbol that the things which unite us are far stronger than the things which would seem to keep us apart'.

EDWARD GARDNER

2011

Before becoming principal conductor of the historic Bergen Philharmonic Orchestra he was Music Director of the English National Opera. This former chorister and student at the Royal Academy of Music enjoys nothing better than an absence of music at home. 'It's funny, but a lot of my life I live in silence,' he once said. 'I don't put music on when I go back to my flat. Silence has become very precious.'

MARIN ALSOP

2013 & 2015

The conductor and violinist became the first woman conductor of the Last Night of the Proms. New Yorker Marin's father was a violinist and her mother a cellist. At the age of nine they took her to see a Leonard Bernstein concert and she was so enraptured that she whispered to her father that she too wanted to conduct. Later, she became a pupil of Bernstein at the Tanglewood Music Center in Boston. She recalls of her Last Night experiences:

'The first occasion that I conducted the Last Night I felt the excitement of the newness of it. But then the second occasion was a little bit harder because I knew what was coming. So it was both easier and more difficult. But all I can say is that I hope there's a third time and maybe the third time is the one where you feel really at home!'

SAKARI ORAMO

2014, 2016 & 2017

Born in Helsinki, he began his musical career as a violinist and later conducted the Finnish Radio Symphony Orchestra. In 2012 he became principal conductor of the BBC SO and delighted Prommers at his first Last Night when he wore a Union flag waistcoat. He began his speech, 'I'm Finnish. We don't talk very much.'

'It's quite inspiring to be able to address a really huge audience by the way of a speech, which conductors like me don't normally do. With the speech you can inspire people, you can touch their hearts and that's always good. But I am very careful with the balance of the speech. I am there as a musician and as a conductor, so you have to speak about things that relate to that'

– Sakari Oramo, Chief Conductor, BBC Symphony Orchestra

PARTY TIME

For current BBC Proms Director, David Pickard, the Last Night has a welcome party feel that he looks forward to being a part of …

'The Last Night is a marvellous tradition that has gone down the ages as being the final party at the end of the season. I think people see it from all sorts of different levels but, I have to say that for those of us working on the Proms, it is precisely that. Everyone has been working so incredibly hard for the previous two months and the Last Night is the chance where we can celebrate everything that we have achieved in that season.

'I think that mixture in the Last Night of tradition and innovation is very much a part of its DNA. Yes, there is the familiarity of the sequence that happens at the end of the concert but it has also always had something contemporary and unusual in it. In a way it is a distillation of everything that has happened beforehand.'

THE WOODEN BATON

Henry Wood was famous for his attention to detail, and this was also directed at his batons, for which he had strict specifications. As he only had a very limited number of rehearsals for each prom, he was keen to ensure that his baton was easily visible and his conducting technique clear and easy to understand. And so he was particular about its length and its colour, and he wrote to the manufacturer, Palmer's of Great Yarmouth, with these specifications:

Weight: slightly under one ounce

Length of handle: 5ins

Length of exposed shaft: 19ins

Total length: 24ins

The shaft was made of seasoned straight-grain poplar wood, carefully riven by hand to ensure that the grain ran straight, and painted white with two coats of water paint. The shaft ran right through the handle.

Not all conductors are so particular about their batons, as Sakari Oramo explains:

'I have several batons and I choose them according to the mood of the day. I have some that are longer and some that are a little bit shorter, but there is no big difference. Some are made of wood and the modern ones are made of carbon fibre with a wooden handle. Wood tends to bend a little, but carbon fibre is great because it doesn't break and it keeps straight.'

DADDY'S GIRL

Last Night conductor Marin Alsop feels particularly close to her late father whenever she picks up one of her batons – because he made them for her.

'My father, who was a violinist, made my conducting batons for me and so they are very special. All of them. I always think of him, especially on important historic occasions like conducting the Last Night of the Proms.

'It began when I couldn't find the guy who had made some earlier batons for me and my father said, "Oh, let me see that. I think I can copy it." This was early on in my career and he said, "How many will you need? Just in case something happens to me?" So he made me about 40 of them! It became a little bit of a joke because he would make them for me at Christmas, and then he would put fake jewels in the end of the handle and stuff like that. It was really cute. Once he even made me an all-gold one. He was very funny. He died in 2014, but I think of him when I am conducting with his batons all the time and he would have loved the Last Nights for sure.'

A BRUSH WITH TALENT

Sir Henry wasn't only a master with the baton – he was pretty handy with a paintbrush too. He attended evening classes at Heatherley's School of Art, near Oxford Street. The Henry Wood Room at the Royal Academy of Music houses a collection of his paintings. They include still lives and several landscapes, particularly of moors and of boating scenes around Portsmouth and the Isle of Wight.

WOOD BY NAME . . .

Another creative outlet for the talented Henry Wood was carpentry. At his country home, Appletree Farm House in Hertfordshire, there was a large barn in the grounds. Inside was a piano, an easel and a carpenter's bench. Sir Henry told an interviewer: 'Carpentering is a complete rest and yet a hobby which keeps you fit.'

WHAT A TURNIP!

Sir Henry Wood's chronometer, or early stopwatch, is among the collection housed at the Academy and was donated by Mrs Tanya Cardew, Sir Henry's daughter, in 1992. It has a heavy silver case with gold liner and was used by the conductor to keep musical time. For reasons known only to Sir Henry, he called it his 'turnip'.

'I love things that break the ice in concerts. I love it when the audience feels confident enough to respond. When that happens, you know the evening is going to be a good one'

— **Roger Norrington, conductor**

THE CONDUCTOR'S SPEECH

The conductor's Last Night speech towards the end of the evening has become very much part of tradition. The usual ingredients are thank yous to the musicians, singers and the audience; the amount raised by Promenaders to support musical charities; the enjoyment throughout the whole

Proms season; a word or two about next year's Proms and, of course, some amusing lines to get the audience chuckling. There have occasionally been some outspoken political or controversial moments.

The tradition dates back to 1941 when Henry Wood gave the first such speech at the close of that season, which was the first at the Royal Albert Hall, when he thanked colleagues and sponsors. But, once again, it was Malcolm Sargent who added the fun and jokey rapport with Promenaders to the speech.

Can you hear me at the back? Good. Here are some of the most memorable excerpts from the speeches of the past.

MALCOLM SARGENT (1957)

'Young ladies, young gentlemen. We have come to the end … We have come to the end of the 63rd season of Henry Wood Promenade Concerts and I want, first of all, because I usually forget, I want first of all to thank you Promenaders so much for these floral tributes, for the lovely buttonholes you've bedecked the orchestra with. I've never seen them look more attractive. And above all for this very kind gift, this cheque you've given me to pass on to the Musicians' Benevolent Fund. Your generosity is almost equal to your good looks.'

DAVID ROBERTSON (2009)

'You may not know this, but when I was 18 I was transplanted as a student from southern California to London, where I learned all sorts of things at the Royal Academy of Music, including adverbs. Somehow they haven't reached the west coast of the United States yet. And once I remember actually being in a room at the Royal Academy of Music with the bust of Henry Wood. And it was just the two of us. He didn't say very much but I felt his imposing figure.'

BIRTHDAY SURPRISE

Malcolm Sargent was born to conduct at the Last Night. He was born in 1895, the year in which the Promenade Concerts began. He later joked in one of his Last Night speeches that Sir Henry Wood, hearing of his birth, had created the Proms so as 'to give me something to do when I grew up'.

MARIN ALSOP (2013)

'And this evening gives us an opportunity to pay tribute to the founder conductor of the Proms, Sir Henry Wood, who's looking down upon us. I feel certain that he would see this evening as a natural progression towards more inclusion within classical music, wouldn't you agree? Now, quite a lot has been made of me being the first woman to conduct the Last Night of the Proms. Thank you, I'm incredibly honoured and proud to have this title, but I have to say I'm still quite shocked that it's 2013 and that there can be firsts for women.'

SAKARI ORAMO (2017)

'"I'm the conductor." "So? Where's your bus?" I first became aware of this joke during my years in Birmingham. It opened my eyes to the multiple meanings of the word "conductor" in English.'

A MOVING NOTE

The Last Night of 1997 was a sombre affair, as were the days leading up to it. The musical offering was changed following the tragic death of Diana, Princess of Wales.

The night before, a special prom was held in memory of her in which one of her favourite classical scores, Verdi's *Requiem*, was played. In another sad note, it was due to be conducted by Georg Solti but he had died a few days earlier, a month before his eighty-fifth birthday, so Colin Davis took his place and the concert was jointly dedicated to Diana and Solti.

On the Last Night itself, John Adams's *Short Ride in a Fast Machine* was dropped due to its inappropriate title at such a time and was replaced by another of the Princess's favourites – 'Jupiter' from Gustav Holst's *The Planets*.

Sir Andrew Davis, who was on Last Night conducting duties, recalls:

> 'The Last Night took place two weeks after Princess Diana and, of course, it was a very traumatic time for the country.

'As it happened, two other notable people died during those two weeks – Mother Teresa and Sir Georg Solti. And so my closing speech that year was a very serious one in which I talked not just about Diana but the sad loss of all three of them, and, in a way, not that I wanted to detract from Princess Diana, but by bringing the other two people in, it somehow served to hit the right note. It was very hard, too, but very necessary.

'Afterwards, I had many people contacting me by various means, saying that somehow what I had said was enabling them to begin to come to terms with Princess Diana's tragic death. A very nice vicar said to me that if ever I want to come and give a sermon in his church he would welcome me!'

CHAPTER 9

MEMORABLE MOMENTS

'I'd always watched the Last Night of the Proms on TV as a kid. It was a real event in our household and we'd all sit down to watch it as a family. So it's a huge honour to be part of it now and actually be there in the Albert Hall'

– Katie Derham, BBC TV Proms presenter

Fainting mid-performance, vacuum cleaners drowning out the orchestra, fires, downpours and demonstrations … all these and more have taken place over the years. But the show must go on, come hell or high water …

AN OVERNIGHT STAR

A regular Prommer became the star one evening when he unexpectedly took centre stage to sing before the audience.

Patrick McCarthy, a young music student, was enjoying his night at the Proms on 7 August 1974 when one of his favourite baritones, Thomas Allen, fainted under the heat mid-way through singing *Carmina Burana*.

The music stopped as he was carried out. Ironically, his stand-in was also a doctor and was required to give assistance to Allen. As the conductor, André Previn, wondered what to do next, on walked a young man he had never seen before. Previn thought he was about to make an announcement but instead he told Previn, 'I know this piece. I'll do it.' The startled conductor replied, 'Fine.'

McCarthy did indeed know the piece because he had sung it several times before as a student. After Allen had fainted, McCarthy's friends persuaded him to take over. He checked backstage to see if there was a replacement lined up and, after being told that there wasn't, he was lent a jacket, provided with the score and directed towards the stage!

Previn later admitted to being nervous as McCarthy took his place in front of the podium. 'I thought, "What if this guy is a nutter?"' he recalled. As he brought the orchestra once more into life, he just hoped that the young student would be able to sing. To his great relief, McCarthy pulled it off and received rapturous applause. Back home in Brighton, his mother, listening on the radio, couldn't believe her ears when she recognised her son's voice!

FIRE AND WATER

A Proms concert was cancelled at the Royal Albert Hall in 2006 after a fire broke out in a bar in the basement. It set off a sprinkler that leaked water into an electrical room, causing a loss of power.

OFF AIR

Pro-Palestinian demonstrators interrupted a performance by the Israel Philharmonic Orchestra in 2011. Although the orchestra continued throughout the demonstration, it was taken off air on BBC Radio 3.

CARRY ON CLEANING!

The sound of vacuum cleaners was heard above the violins, flutes and horns during perhaps the most bizarre performance at the Last Night of the Proms on Saturday 12 September 2009. But it wasn't because the cleaners had got their timing wrong. The score was Sir Malcolm Arnold's *A Grand, Grand Overture*, which included star turns from special guests on unusual objects.

The BBC Symphony Orchestra's chief conductor Jiří Bělohlávek, violinist Jennifer Pike and pianist Stephen Hough 'played' vacuum cleaners, whilst naturalist Sir David Attenborough made his Proms performance debut on the floor polisher. DJ Goldie, impressionist Rory Bremner, broadcaster Martha Kearney and double bass player Chi-chi Nwanoku accompanied on rifles!

TEARS AND SHIVERS

Paul Hughes, General Manager of the BBC SO and Chorus, and the BBC Singers has been attending the Proms for 20 years and recalls his most spine-tingling moments:

'There was one musical moment in 2017 that took me by surprise. Sakari Oramo was conducting *Finlandia*, which is a well-known piece by Sibelius, but we did it in the choral setting, which isn't heard that often.

The chorus learnt it in Finnish and sang it from memory, and it was intensely moving.

'I was sitting in a box with the Finnish ambassador and other guests, and everybody was in tears. It was extremely emotional to hear that piece by a Finnish composer, led by a Finnish conductor in the centenary year of Finland's independence.

'Another occasion sent a shiver down my spine. Eric Whitacre's *Deep Field* was being performed in 2015, which is about space and is largely an orchestra piece, and then about five minutes before the end of the 25-minute performance, the BBC Symphony Chorus all walked down the aisles around the Albert Hall and they stood in pairs on the steps and sang unaccompanied. They started really quietly and it almost made the hairs on the back of my neck stand up. I'll never forget that. It was very exciting.'

L is for Largo – slow tempo

A is for Allegro – lively tempo

S is for Soprano – the highest female vocal range

T is for Tenor – the highest male voice, between alto and baritone

N is for Natural – indicating that a note is neither sharp nor flat

I is for Instrumentation – the way a composer or arranger takes musical sounds and assigns them to specific instruments

G is for Grace Note – ornamental (embellished) note played before the main note

H is for Harmony – when notes are in consonance

T is for Tonic – the first note in a scale

O is for Octave – the interval between two musical notes, the upper one of which has twice the pitch of the lower one. In a major or minor scale the distance of this interval is eight steps away, hence the term 'octave'.

F is for Forte – loud or strong

T is for Treble – the highest part, voice, instrument or range

H is for Harmonic Progression – movement from one chord to another

E is for Elegy – a mournful, melancholic piece

P is for Piano – gently, soft

R is for Resolution – the move of a note or chord from dissonance (unstable sound) to consonance (calm, agreeable)

O is for Opus – work number of a composition

M is for Motif – a short, melodic pattern or musical idea that runs through a piece

S is for Symphony – an extended musical composition for orchestra, usually in four movements

NIGHT AND DAME

Dame Judi Dench delighted the audience when she sang 'Send in the Clowns' from *A Little Night Music*, a prom in the 2010 season that was devoted to the music of Broadway legend Stephen Sondheim, who was 80 that year.

'Singing at the Proms is not something I ever imagined I would do, and it's a hugely exciting – if slightly daunting – prospect,' she said beforehand. Afterwards she commented, 'A more frightening experience I have yet to have.'

On hearing her performance of the song during the National Theatre's 1995 revival of the show, Sondheim is said to have told the actress, 'It's yours now.'

BRIT-TASTIC!

The singing of 'Rule, Britannia!' has become an ever-more theatrical event. If you really want the crowd behind you, then you'd better dress to impress …

UNDIE-WHELMED

Handsome German tenor Jonas Kaufmann was taken aback at the 2015 Last Night. The singer – dubbed 'Poldark of the Proms' – was pelted with lacy underwear from female Promenaders after a rousing rendition of 'Nessun dorma'.

He took it in good spirit though, laughing and holding a pair up to the audience. Later, as he finished singing 'Rule, Britannia!', he returned the compliment by reaching into the back of his trousers and whipping out a pair of Union flag boxer shorts that he waved in the air before throwing them into the audience.

HALF AND HALF

In 1998, American baritone Thomas Hampson came on to sing 'Rule, Britannia!' wearing a waistcoat – one half of which bore the Stars and Stripes and the other half the Union flag.

'I don't have any memories of watching the Last Night of the Proms when I was a child. I only became aware of it when I started working in the UK and I thought, "Oh gosh. Only the Brits can do this the right way." And I was right. There's something about having fun'

— **Marin Alsop, conductor**

WHO'S QUEEN?

Gwyneth Jones raised a huge cheer on the Last Night in 1991 as she imperiously strode on in full Britannia regalia, adorned with a golden helmet, carrying a trident in one hand and a shield in the other. What the audience couldn't see – and was revealed by the TV cameras – was that Dame Gwyneth had the lyrics of 'Rule, Britannia!' stuck to the back of the shield, in case they slipped her mind.

In 2011 Susan Bullock also dressed as Britannia, carrying a spear instead of a trident, as did Nina Stemme in 2017.

> '"Rule, Britannia!" is a real pig to sing. It's full of twiddly fast notes'
>
> – Susan Bullock, soprano

A FIERY PERFORMANCE

In 1993, Della Jones threw open the train on her blue dress to reveal a white lining with a stunning embroidery of the Welsh dragon.

RULE, WALES!

When Bryn Terfel performed 'Rule, Britannia!' at the Proms in 1994 and 2008, he sang the third verse in Welsh. The first time he walked through the hall to the stage in a Welsh rugby shirt, carrying a rugby ball and Welsh flag and dragon. At the end he kicked the rugby ball into the arena. The audience loved it but Terfel later admitted that he had been wracked with nerves and wanted to run away.

'Before walking out I had cold sweats and shortness of breath,' said Bryn. 'I was so nervous I nearly escaped through the back door!'

As the third Welsh singer in a short period of time, Bryn was keen to make as much of an impression as his compatriots Gwyneth Jones and Della Jones when it came to his costume.

> 'I stupidly kicked the rugby ball – which, by the way, had been signed by all the artists – into the middle of the crowd, narrowly missing one of those expensive revolving cameras that they place in the middle of the Promenaders. After what seemed like an age, there was one Excalibur hand that came out of the crowd to catch it single-handedly and pluck it out of the air. I thought, "Well, somebody has got a nice memento from the Last Night of the Proms."
>
> 'After that, Roger Wright, Director of the BBC Proms at the time, invited me to sing there again and that for me was an incredible highlight, to be invited a second time to do the Last Night of the Proms. Now I am awaiting my hat-trick.'

LORDING IT

Sarah Connolly dressed in full Nelson regalia in 2009. She imperiously handed her tricorn hat to the conductor, David Robertson, to hold before she started!

BANDANITANNIA

For his Last Night appearance in 1999, Jamaican-born opera star Willard White sang 'Rule, Britannia!' with a Union flag wrapped, bandana-style, around his head. He'd earlier applied his cavernous tones to songs from *South Pacific* and *Show Boat*.

CROSS TO BARE

In 2012 Maltese tenor soloist Joseph Calleja came on to sing 'Rule, Britannia!' in a blue Union flag tracksuit, which he unzipped to display a T-shirt bearing the Maltese Cross. He was joined on stage by medal winners from the British Olympic rowing and sailing teams.

FLYING THE FLAG

In 1985 Sarah Walker wore a long, flowing dress in pure white, but there was a surprise in store for the audience when, at the crescendo of 'Rule, Britannia!', she unfastened the left shoulder and pulled back a swathe of white material to reveal a huge Union flag. The show-stopping dress had an unusual provenance – thanks to Dame Edna Everage. Sarah Walker recalls:

> 'The day I got the letter asking me to perform, I was so excited because, let's face it, it's almost better than being asked to do a Royal wedding! I showed it to pianist Graham Johnson, who helped me write the most fantastic letter to Dame Edna. It said something like, "I can only assume I have been asked because you are elsewhere engaged," and asking her for help with a dress that reflected my patriotism and love of my country. Dame

Edna (aka Barry Humphries) wrote me back this lovely letter saying, "Dear Dame Sarah. How sweet of you to write and ask my advice." She said she'd ask her son Kenny – a fashion designer – but if that failed, she told me to go to St John Roper, who made her famous Sydney Opera House dress and the baked bean dress she wore to the Heinz factory.

'I knew what I wanted, because I like designing things, so they made it. It was a white dress that looked a bit like a toga, so it had a Grecian effect. And when you pulled the rip cord, so to speak, out came this giant flag. It brought the house down.'

The triumphant unfurling, however, almost didn't happen:

'The night before the Proms, I picked up the dress and decided I should try it on at home just to make sure everything worked properly – and he had put the flag on the wrong way! The flag was width-ways, so that I would have had to have an eight-foot-long arm to hold it out, instead of lengthways. So I rang them the following morning and they readjusted it at the last minute.'

Four years later, she sang the song in a red, white and blue striped dress, which she designed herself. Once again, it had been specially adapted and, at the crucial moment, she unhooked the sleeves and they opened up to depict two large Union flags:

'The second one was even more fun and I knew exactly what I wanted to wear. I got the idea from an evening dress I saw on Miss World. This was in the days when they all had *Dynasty* shoulders and I thought it would work well, so I got my dressmaker to make that. That one was a red, white and blue tricolour – with the Union flags hidden in the shoulder pads – but I didn't really pick up on the significance of the French flag look until I got there and realised that year had been French year, highlighting a lot of French music at the Proms.'

Her iconic white dress, worn in 1985, was put to excellent use after its debut appearance. She recalls:

'When I began to think of retirement I had a huge wardrobe of concert dresses, numbering probably 150 or more, most of which probably didn't fit me by then. So I would have dress sales every now and then, usually in the wardrobe at the Royal Opera House because the ladies in the chorus, who were all good friends, would fall on them like locusts. During one of the last sales I had, the guy who worked in the accounts – who was about six foot six and had amazingly peroxided hair – bought my first Proms dress. It was perfect for him because he did a drag act round the corner! He may still be wearing it today.'

CONDUCTING BANTER

Promenaders like a laugh, and so conductors who strike up a rapport with them and share a joke are always warmly appreciated.

GOING FOR A SONG

Andrew Davis set the bar high when he made his conductor's closing speech in 1992. He sang it to the tune of 'The Major-General's Song' from Gilbert and Sullivan's *Pirates of Penzance*! He rhymed 'festival' with the antiquated word 'aestival', which means pertaining to summer.

It began:

'This is the very model of a modern music festival;
    With entertainment sonet, promenadable and aestival.'

He recalled:

'I'd been doing the speech for several consecutive years at that point and I was saying to my wife, "Oh dear. What am I going to say in my speech this year? I can't keep saying the same old thing." And she said, "Why don't you sing it?" And so I sang it to "The Major-General's Song" and, I must say, it was quite clever really – he said, modestly!

'Then, of course, the year after that I thought, "Oh Lord, the speech is going to be boring now!"

I couldn't sing it again. It's the kind of thing you can only do once.'

THE PROMS WITHOUT AN ORCHESTRA

'The combined distractions of two World Wars failed to stop the Henry Wood Promenade Concert but this summer, which can bring nothing but sorrow to all concerned, things are different'

– Adrian Boult, conductor

The 1980 Proms nearly did not take place. A decline in the UK economy in the 1970s put the BBC budgets under strain, and the difficult decision was taken to disband the BBC Scottish Symphony Orchestra, BBC Northern Ireland (Ulster) Orchestra and three UK regional orchestras to save £130m.

It was met with strike action by the Musicians' Union. When conciliatory talks failed to get anywhere, the BBC cancelled the first night of the Proms. Two following prom nights were also cancelled.

In the early hours of Thursday 24 July, an agreement was made between the BBC and the Musicians' Union. It was formally approved by both on 2 August and the strike was ended. The deal saved three of the threatened orchestras – the BBC Scottish Symphony, the BBC Northern Ireland Orchestra and the London Studio Players.

The BBC Proms resumed on Thursday 7 August, three weeks late. Twenty of the 57 scheduled concerts had been cancelled.

THE ENTERTAINER

Violinist Nigel Kennedy was full of high jinks at the Last Night in 2013. He ambled on stage wearing an Aston Villa football shirt and carrying a mug of tea. Throughout his very individual recital of Monti's *Csárdás* he kept conductor Marin Alsop and the BBC Symphony Orchestra on their toes trying to follow him.

He added flourishes, interjected various other pieces of music, paused to pop balloons tied to the podium with his bow and blew kisses to his fellow musicians. BBC commentator Katie Derham said that Marin Alsop had done 'fabulously well' to keep up with Kennedy's antics, adding: 'Nigel Kennedy could not have pleased the audience more. You have to be really, really good to be able to muck around that much. I think he loves Aston Villa almost as much as he loves winding up conductors.'

Marin was equally amused by his gags.

'That was fun, and possibly the only moment that really shocked me was when Nigel came out in the second half wearing a football shirt and carrying a cup of tea,' she recalled.

A PROM FIRST

Marin Alsop became a groundbreaker when she became the first woman to conduct at the Last Night, in 2013.

'I found conducting the Last Night to be a very emotional evening because it represented a lot of different things to a lot of different people. I think for the prom audience it was meaningful that I was the first woman to conduct the occasion and they decked out my podium in the interval with pink balloons that said "It's a girl." I thought it was really funny and very much in the spirit of the Last Night.

'For me, the occasion was about my relationship with the UK. The Last Night of the Proms represents something very special for the people of Britain, and to be invited to host the evening as the conductor is a great honour in terms of my relationship with the public especially, and the musicians, of course.

'I have felt a warmth and a connection ever since I first started conducting in Britain. I don't know exactly why it has been so strong. Maybe it's a shared work ethic. The British musicians work so hard and the British people work so hard but they also know how to have a good laugh. They have a great sense of humour and I just had a real deep connection.

'So for me personally, conducting the Last Night was about that deep connection I've always felt to the country and people. Then of course there was the added excitement of being the first woman. That became a symbol for many people in breaking some barriers, about people aspiring to do something that they hadn't been able to do before. It became a vehicle for people to have hope, I think.'

Bryn Terfel, who has sung at two Last Nights, explains why he thinks the occasion holds such a warm place in the hearts of the nation.

'First of all, it's a series of concerts for an incredible amount of weeks of classical music that is untouched by any other festival during the summer – the number of performers, the orchestras, conductors, pianists, singers ... you name it. And they are even branching out into having some different types of evenings, like *Strictly Come Dancing* and the music from *Star Wars*. It's just an incredible festival that you always want to be a part of and you'd love to think that you as a performer would be in the Proms every year. Sadly that's never going to be the case, but I distinctly remember the first time that I got an invitation to come and sing at the Proms. I was really excited.

'On top of being such an amazing and important series of concerts for the UK, it's something that people travel to, worldwide, to hear these incredible performers on such an incredible stage, because that's something you've only ever been able to imagine. The Albert Hall is quite a stage for all performers all through the year and that the Proms can take it over for that number of weeks and to fill it daily and sometimes twice in a day is wonderful. It's unique and, for me, the prospect of singing there is incredible.'

WATER, WATER, EVERYWHERE

In 2009, as the players of the Vienna Philharmonic were packing up after their Prom, a departing double bassist knocked a sprinkler head in the bull run under the stage and water poured from the ceiling onto the cherished instruments below. The stopcock was eventually located, but all hands were commandeered to mop up before cellist Yo-Yo Ma's late-night prom, including those of BBC Proms Director Roger Wright himself.

HERE'S ONE I SANG EARLIER

Blue Peter presenters enjoy a challenge and Janet Ellis certainly faced one when she auditioned to sing with the BBC Symphony Chorus at the Last Night of the Proms in 1985. She was filmed throughout the rehearsal period. 'Performing at the Last Night of the Proms was the high-light of my career,' she later claimed.

In 2010 there were two Last Nights. A week before the usual one was a recreation of the Last Night from 1910. It was a revelation to many because of the absence of 'Land of Hope and Glory' and 'Jerusalem'. *Lamia* by Dorothy Howell was played in honour of Henry Wood, who had championed her.

The event took place on Sunday 5 September 2010 at the Albert Hall. Included in the programme were *Fantasia on British Sea-Songs* and Elgar's *Pomp and Circumstance March No. 4*.

Anyone expecting the conductor's speech at the end of the prom was also in for a surprise. Paul Daniel just gave a brief word, explaining that there were no speeches back then.

PERUVIAN PAIR

Peruvian tenor Juan Diego Flórez sang 'Rule, Britannia!' dressed in a fabulous Inca chief costume in 2016, with feathered headwear and carrying a ceremonial axe, complete with large metal disc earrings. Conductor Sakari Oramo bowed to him in a 'hailing' fashion.

Earlier in the evening, dressed in a more sober suit to sing arias by Rossini and Donizetti, somebody threw him a cuddly Paddington Bear (another visitor to London from Peru). He serenaded it during a performance of 'Guantanamera' – part of a medley of popular Latin songs.

'He is as Peruvian as me,' he told the audience. 'You know, he was found in Paddington Station … Nobody in Peru knows about this. Anyway, I know him. I love him.'

JOIN IN OR CHILL OUT

The BBC's first ever Relaxed Prom in 2017 was suitable for children and adults with autism, sensory and communication impairments and learning disabilities, as well as the deaf, hard of hearing, blind and partially sighted.

The fun and interactive musical experience provided plenty of opportunities for participation, singing, dancing and moving around. 'Chill-out' spaces outside the auditorium were also available.

The prom featured picture communication systems projected onto large screens, as well as audio description and British sign language interpretation.

The programme included Rimsky-Korsakov's *Flight of the Bumblebee*, Rossini's *William Tell* overture, as well as Pharrell Williams's 'Happy' and the theme from *Doctor Who*.

BBC Proms Director David Pickard explained that it was set up so that 'everyone feels comfortable'. He added, 'The whole format is different. It is relaxed in terms of the way it's presented, and we're very careful about the lighting and the noise because there are all sorts of things people with impairments can find challenging.'

A VINTAGE PERFORMANCE

Sir Neville Marriner became the oldest conductor of a prom at the age of 90 in 2014. He had first appeared at the Proms in 1963 as a violinist and later as a conductor in 1997.

He conducted Beethoven's First Symphony and Bruch's Violin Concerto No. 1, along with an arrangement of Walton's *Suite from Henry V*, and was joined by actor John Hurt, narrating the words of Shakespeare for the BBC Proms audience.

'What remains magical for me about the BBC Proms is that sense of communal listening, particularly in that unique round building, but also the audience community experiencing the concerts on BBC Radio 3, BBC TV and online. There is a palpable sense of us all continuing on our journey of musical discovery – of familiar works in fresh interpretations, performers making their debuts and being introduced to a wide audience, new music specially commissioned for the Proms or pieces that have yet to be heard in the UK. Commentators often say how remarkable the Proms audience is. And performers have often asked me if they can take the audience with them to all their concerts, as they get so much electricity and inspiration from them'

– Roger Wright, Director of the BBC Proms 2008–14

GOING INTERNATIONAL

The BBC Proms started to look overseas from 1966, starting with the Moscow Radio Symphony Orchestra, which was the first foreign orchestra to play at the festival. The ensemble performed Britten's *The Young Person's Guide to the Orchestra*, Shostakovich's Cello Concerto No. 1 and Tchaikovsky's *Manfred*.

They were followed by the Polish Radio Symphony Orchestra in 1967 and the Czech Philharmonic Orchestra in 1969.

EVERYONE'S A CRITIC

The Proms have a long history of adventurous and avant-garde music going all the way back to Henry Wood's tenure. But it has not always been well received ...

HISS – TORY

Wood's passion for new music was not shared by the Queen's Hall audience at the 1912 Proms. Neither was it a favourite of the Queen's Hall Orchestra.

The premiere of Arnold Schoenberg's *Five Pieces for Orchestra* left many scratching their heads in bewilderment, others openly hissing, some thinking it was a joke and critics apoplectic with anger.

The Austrian composer was in the vanguard of the expressionist movement and his music disregarded key, resulting in atonality, with instruments often played at the extreme of their registers. Audiences and critics found the concept difficult to understand. There was so much unrest at one concert that the police were called!

Five Pieces for Orchestra was completed in 1909. Schoenberg described it as 'a vivid, uninterrupted succession of colours and moods', with 'no architecture, no construction'.

During rehearsals the Queen's Hall Orchestra struggled with the technical challenges and Wood urged them to persevere, with the words: 'Stick to it, gentlemen – this is nothing to what you will have to play in 25 years' time!'

When it was premiered the audience was duly startled and shocked by it. The critics managed to collect their thoughts into some scathing reviews. *The Referee* described it as 'formless, incoherent, disjointed ideas of what constitutes music'.

'The sounds of nature in their crudest form', said a prim review in the *Morning Post*, whilst to *The Globe* it brought to mind 'the dismal wailings of a tortured soul'.

MAD MAX

Lancashire-born composer Peter Maxwell Davies, who was known as Max, managed to clear half of the audience when his 40-minute piece, *Worldes Blis*, had its world premiere at the 1969 Proms.

A leading light of contemporary music, Max took a phlegmatic stance to the hostile reaction. After all, maybe the audience wasn't ready for seven percussionists whacking metal scaffolding joining the more familiar instruments of the orchestra.

Hundreds walked out. The music critic Tom Service later described the event to be 'as near as the Royal Albert Hall has ever come to a riot'.

Max himself recalled, 'Most of the audience walked out, and most of those who stayed booed.' He explained that 'a very special sort of listening is required. The whole experience of *Worldes Blis* is a very dark one and that may have made it out of place at a prom.'

NO NEED TO PANIC

Harrison Birtwistle's 1995 score, *Panic*, was premiered in the second half of the Last Night of the Proms in 2007. The contemporary piece baffled a few in the Albert Hall, but many watching and listening at home on TV were outraged by its inclusion before the patriotic favourites. The BBC switchboard was jammed with people ringing up to complain.

'The Harrison Birtwistle piece was a disgrace and an insult to the British public,' stormed one viewer. And critics in the popular press joined in with the insults, with the *Daily Mail* calling it 'a horrible cacophony' and the *Daily Express* 'unmitigated rubbish'!

CHAPTER 10

AROUND THE COUNTRY

'It is good for the Proms to occasionally leave the mother ship of the Royal Albert Hall and go off to other interesting places to make music'

– David Pickard, Director of the BBC Proms

Henry Wood's original mission was to bring music to the masses. The same goal was behind the idea of taking the Proms out of the Albert Hall to various places around the country, as well as Proms in the Park, which enabled more people than ever to experience live Proms.

SPREADING THE MUSIC

The popularity of the Last Night led to the first Prom in the Park, which took place in Hyde Park in 1996. This meant that those who were unable to get a ticket to the Albert Hall could get a share of the Promenading experience.

A review of the 1996 prom in Hyde Park in the *Guardian* newspaper described the scene thus: 'Surging crowds, rows of fast-food trucks, makeshift stalls and a large concave auditorium flanked by huge video screens. Jean Sibelius stole the air. It was 5pm on Saturday, and as Sir Colin Davis led the European Union Youth Orchestra through the Second Symphony's epic coda, Concorde roared overhead.'

Crackerjack presenter Ed Stewart introduced what the *Guardian* described as 'sna███████dards' from the Piccadilly Dance Orchestra, █████████e 'lusty singing' by the Maesteg an████████oir and a 'highly entertaining sequence'████████group Cantabile.

The evening's music was broadcast live on BBC Radio 2 and featured the BBC Concert Orchestra under Robert Stapleton. It included Bernstein's *Candide* overture, Sarasate's *Carmen Fantasy*, featuring James Galway playing 'Gypsy Dance'. Pianist-sisters Katia and Marielle Labèque played a selection from *West Side Story* and soprano Maria Ewing's strong voice did justice to an open-air performance of 'Una voce poco fa' from *The Barber of Seville* and 'Vissi d'arte' from *Tosca*. Later she returned with crowd-pleasers such as a Broadway sequence that included songs by the likes of Gershwin and Coward.

After a brief interval it was time to link up with the Albert Hall for the second half of the proceedings. Conductor Andrew Davis appeared on huge screens and the outdoors audience was delighted by the audio quality as they heard the BBC SO play Malcolm Arnold's *The Sound Barrier*.

Shouts and whistles greeted the arrival of the 'blockbusters' – 'Land of Hope and Glory', 'Sea-Songs', 'Rule, Britannia!' and 'Jerusalem' – as the 25,000-strong crowd heartily sang along. The experiment was judged to be a success and it was to become the newest staple of the ever-developing BBC Proms.

FROM RABBLE-ROUSING TO JOY UNCONFINED

The Prom in the Park idea had been discussed in the early 1990s but the then Director of the BBC Proms, John Drummond, was set against it. He disliked the nature of the Last Night anyway, and complained that it would detract from the main event in the Albert Hall and reduce the demand for tickets. He added, for good measure, that such an open-air concert was 'the essence of mindless populism imposed on an event which is already dangerously rabble-rousing'.

In contrast, Nicholas Kenyon, who succeeded Drummond in 1996, enthusiastically championed the idea and embraced the Last Night crowd-pleasing favourites.

'I am a "Let joy be unconfined" man myself,' he told the press. And the open-air Hyde Park concert went ahead.

CHAMBER MUSIC

In that same year, 1996, a related series of eight lunchtime chamber concerts began, taking place on Mondays during the Proms season. In their first year they were held in the Britten Hall of the Royal College of Music, just across the road from the Albert Hall. This provided a more intimate venue for music not suitable for the cavernous Albert Hall.

The following year they moved to the Henry Cole lecture theatre at the Victoria and Albert Museum. In 2005 they moved again, to the new Cadogan Hall, just off London's Sloane Square.

PROMS PLUS

2011 saw the introduction of Proms Plus, which have become a much-loved addition to the season, enabling visitors to enrich their understanding of music and the arts in general.

The free daily events take place at various locations, including the Elgar Room in the Albert Hall, the Royal College of Music, Cadogan Hall and Imperial College's student union, and feature various talks, performances, workshops and family events.

WIDER STILL AND WIDER

In subsequent years, Proms in the Park events have extended to Belfast, Glasgow, Swansea, Manchester and Enniskillen, thus giving the night more of an encompassing United Kingdom feel, rather than an English-centric one. Each location typically plays the country's national anthem before the link-up with the Albert Hall, where English, Welsh, Scottish and Irish melodies are often added to the 'Sea-Songs'.

'We wanted to make the Last Night as inclusive as possible and the most appealing way to do it was around the four nations,' said Kenyon.

'The Proms in the Park has really broadened the event. It's made far more people aware of it. I think it's done a very good job in that respect. It's taken it to

different parts of the country to people
who wouldn't necessarily be able to come
to London, even though they could watch
on TV or listen on radio. Radio 2 joins
Radio 3 to broadcast the concert'

– Helen Heslop, BBC Live Events team manager

PLENTY OF PARKING SPACE

The desire to take the Proms out of the Albert Hall and
to different, unlikely places probably reached its zenith in
2016 with a prom at a multi-storey car park in Peckham,
South East London.

The prom was held in celebration of American mini-
malist composer Steve Reich's 80th birthday, and his works
were played by Christopher Stark and the Multi-Story
Orchestra, conducted by Stark. It included Reich's first
major work for a full orchestra, *Music for Large Ensemble*,
and the single-movement 'octet' *Eight Lines*.

The 'Proms in the car park' was the idea of David
Pickard, who had been appointed the new Director of the
BBC Proms towards the end of 2015:

'I introduced this idea of taking the Proms to some
unlikely venues in my first year. In a way it was harking
back to an older tradition where the Proms were, for
a time, outside of the Albert Hall. I didn't want all
the Proms to take place in South Kensington.

'London is a very big and diverse place and in my first year we found that if you go to somewhere like the car park in Peckham, you get a different sort of audience and, given that the Proms are about bringing classical music to the widest possible audience, that was an important thing to me, to reach out to a different set of people. But also it was about finding spaces where the music would be heard in a different way. It is slightly bizarre hearing trains rattling down below you through Peckham Rye station, but actually, it becomes part of the experience. It gives you a different feel for it.'

The Proms returned to the Peckham car park in 2017 to join Christopher Stark and the Multi-Story Orchestra for a concert rooted in the sounds and communities of the city. The music included John Adams's metallic *Harmonielehre* and Kate Whitley's 'I am I say', written for local schoolchildren. The concert opened with Bach's *Wachet auf, ruft uns die Stimme*.

IF MUSIC BE THE FOOD OF LOVE ...

In contrast to the cold concrete of the car park, David Pickard also took the Proms to the cosy warmth and beautiful, candle-lit setting of the Sam Wanamaker Playhouse at Shakespeare's Globe in 2016, where the ensemble orchestra Arcangelo played early music inspired by works of Shakespeare. It included Purcell's *Dance for the Haymakers* and Locke's *Dance of the Fantastick Spirits*.

'It was perfect to go and hear that music by candlelight in a tiny venue in a way that probably wouldn't have been so special in the Albert Hall, which is really too big for that music,' says Pickard.

Musical Director of Arcangelo Jonathan Cohen loved the venue. 'It's a lovely little theatre which is made of wood, so the sound is very exact and real. We can all hear each other,' he said. 'You can smell the wood and feel the way the sound is bouncing around in a very realistic, almost direct manner. It really makes the experience of performing on stage there alive and unique.'

Soprano Katharine Watson, added, 'The candlelight creates a very intimate feeling and a soft ambience that really charges the atmosphere.'

OUT OF LONDON

In 2017, for the first time in 90 years, the Proms left London and a concert was played at Hull, that year's City of Culture, with music inspired by water.

The stage was on the dock, looking out to sea, and the performance centred on Handel's *Water Music*, first performed 300 years earlier at a river party for George I on the Thames.

Nicholas McGegan directed the Royal Northern Sinfonia in a programme featuring everything from storms and shipwrecks to calm seas and seductive sirens. Among the pieces played were Mendelssohn's *Calm Sea and Prosperous Voyage* and Grace Williams's *Sea Sketches*.

The trend for taking the Proms around the country continues under Pickard's direction with a performance in

Lincoln in 2018 to mark 100 years since the end of the First World War, with a piece by Stravinsky, *The Soldier's Tale*, which was written in the year that the war ended.

'We were looking for a venue that had a First World War feel to it, and we found a drill hall, which is now an arts centre in Lincoln,' he says. 'To me that's perfect, because you are in a venue that feels like it's the right place and is appropriate for the piece. Also, I think it's great to take the Proms to somewhere like Lincoln, which is not necessarily the place where you would expect the Proms to go.

'For me, it's an interesting idea to take it to parts of the United Kingdom that surprise people. It's a strand that I would like to continue.'

LOGISTICAL NIGHTMARE

As manager of the Live Events team putting together the BBC Proms, Helen Heslop faces logistical hell and, despite her enthusiasm for the Proms in the Parks, they have done nothing to ease her working day:

'In the second half, when they link up with the Albert Hall, there is time pressure. You've got these four other parks and the music there has to finish at 10.30pm. These restrictions are in place because of nearby residents, so it's all about getting the timings right.

'In 2017, for example, we finished almost too early because we were so worried about it. We kept it tight and finished about sixteen minutes past ten, whereas in the previous year we went past 10.30. It's hard to plan because of variables, such as the conductor's speech. You might plan for x number of minutes, and some of them stick to it and some of them don't. You can't do anything about that.

'The other big challenge is the tie-ups of the parks in terms of the technical aspect, like when we are having to pipe what we're recording back into the Hall and broadcasting on TV and radio. My wonderful technical colleagues make that happen but it's sometimes tricky to manage it.'

'It's a great thing that the Proms don't limit themselves to the Albert Hall. The Chamber Proms at the Cadogan Hall have been very successful, as have the other venues, and Hyde Park and all the Proms in the Parks work well in the summer. I am all for widening the scope of the Proms. It can only be a good thing because the Proms are a great brand with which you can make classical music known to wider audiences'
— **Sakari Oramo, Chief Conductor, BBC Symphony Orchestra**

CHAPTER 11

THEMED
PROMS

'The Proms are about the communication between the stage and the audience. It has something to do with the fact that you've got all the people who have paid the least standing right in the middle'

– Nicholas Kenyon, Director of the BBC Proms 1996–2007

The traditional Proms ethos, stretching back to Sir Henry Wood, has always been to encourage people from all backgrounds to listen to classical music. This has led to many and varied themed Proms over the years to attract all ages and social groups. The boundaries have been extended to include everything from rock music to grime and even comedy.

OUT OF AFRICA

Sengalese singer, guitarist and composer Baaba Maal raised the temperature with his music in 2005, when the annual world music prom was devoted to Africa.

He began by sitting on a carved wooden throne, strumming his guitar and then explained that, similar to a tribal setting, more and more people would join him as the evening progressed. These included musicians, dancers, the African Children's Choir and Maal's band, Daande

Lenol. At the end of an exhilarating evening the audience roared its approval.

COMEDY PROM

Tim Minchin proved to be an engaging host for the first ever Comedy Prom in 2011, cleverly disarming any critics from the outset. The Australian comedian and musician began proceedings by sitting in the audience, dressed in a grey suit, wig and fake beard, and sang:

'I sit here, as for 20 years I've sat,
wearing my music critic's hat.
I mean it's clearly not an actual hat.
It's metaphorical.
And in those 20 years I'm sad
to say these wondrous promenades have gone
from bad to worse to bad,
to pretty crap to bloody horrible.
I admit, I'm a bit of a classical music boffin
and although I've said this often,
the final nail in the coffin
of these Proms is surely imminent.
Yes, we survived Nigel effing Kennedy,
but surely there's no earthly remedy
for a night of so-called comedy
hosted by an immigrant.'

Contributors included Sue Perkins, cabaret duo Kit and the Widow, mime artist The Boy with Tape on His

Face – who manically mimed a routine to the *William Tell* overture, racing hand-held horses on sticks, and rapper Doc Brown, who rapped about how he wished David Attenborough were his grandfather!

HUMANS AND A SCRAP METAL ORCHESTRA

The music behind the acclaimed BBC TV documentary series *Human Planet*, about how humans adapt to their environment, took centre stage in 2011.

Nitin Sawhney's beautiful and often dramatic scores were played by musicians from around the world to footage from the series showing on a giant screen. The tone later changed for an intriguing and amusing addition to the entertainment.

A BBC Four project called *Scrapheap Orchestra* had seen conductor Charles Hazlewood challenge top instrument-makers to remake a whole orchestra from scrap. Now the instruments were about to be played at the prestigious Royal Albert Hall by top musicians.

Hazlewood introduced some of the instruments, which included a cello made of plywood and two washing-up bowls, a double bass from parts of a car, a white bassoon taken from a shower cubicle, a tuba from a ventilation duct and a violin from a piece of toilet wastepipe with a bow that had once been an arrow! The BBC Concert Orchestra rose magnificently to the challenge to use these scrapyard instruments to play Tchaikovsky's *1812 Overture*.

PASTA JOKE

The Spaghetti Western Orchestra Prom in 2011 featured five musicians from Australia who joyously celebrated their love of the music of Ennio Morricone in spaghetti western movies such as *The Good, the Bad and the Ugly*.

They re-created the sounds on conventional instruments as well as some extraordinary ones, such as cereal packets, an asthma inhaler, rubber gloves, beer bottles and a pack of playing cards.

CRACKING, PROM-IT!

Wallace unveiled his musical marvel, *Concerto in Ee Lad*, to a delighted audience of all ages at the 2012 Wallace & Gromit Prom.

But before the concerto, conductor Nicholas Collon, who was gamely working his way through a programme of music leading to the big event, was continually interrupted by the ringing of a red telephone next to him. It was Wallace and, as everyone saw on the screen, his final preparations on his customised piano were not going well. But, as usual, his faithful pooch Gromit got him out of a sticky situation. Before you could say 'cracking cheese', Gromit had penned a brand-new concerto for violin and dog, leaving Wallace the comparatively simple job of clashing a cymbal, which he managed not to muck up!

The second half saw a screening of Nick Park's animated film *A Matter of Loaf and Death*, shown for the first time with a live orchestral soundtrack. The familiar invigorating theme tune had everyone smiling and clapping along to the beat, eagerly looking forward to what was to come.

IN GOD'S NAME

The London Adventist Chorale, London Community Gospel Choir, People's Christian Fellowship Choir, Muyiwa & Riversongz and Pastor David Daniel raised the roof of the Royal Albert Hall in 2013 at the second Gospel Prom.

Leading vocal ensembles combined with community choirs and soloists including Stuart K. Hine, Carla Ellington and Patsy Ford to sing such favourites as 'How Great Thou Art', 'Swing Low, Sweet Chariot','O Happy Day' and 'Amazing Grace'.

The prom was considered to be such a success that three years later there was another one. The evening was hosted by Former Destiny's Child singer Michelle Williams. Noel Robinson and Nu Image, accompanied by the University Gospel Choir of the Year Mass Choir, kicked things off with the energetic 'Freedom', before seguing neatly into the plaintive 'Rain'.

Other artists included singer Israel J. Allen and saxophonist YolanDa Brown. At the end, soloists and choirs came together to form an elite gospel 'superchoir'.

FROM HIP-OP TO GRIME

Following 2013's Urban Classic Prom, BBC Radio 1Xtra presented a celebration of the thriving urban music scene, from hip-hop to grime, in 2015. Some of the best-known urban artists joined presenters MistaJam and Sian Anderson on stage. Jules Buckley once again conducted.

Stormzy confidently bounded on stage to perform 'Know Me From' and Krept & Konan got the Proms in party spirit with their hit 'Freak of the Week', whilst grime veteran Lethal Bizzle powered his way through his medley.

A BOLLY-GOOD SHOW

Emeli Sandé and Kanika Kapoor were special guests for a night of Bollywood and bhangra music at the Asian Network Prom in 2015, marking the 50th anniversary of Asian programmes on the BBC. Bobby Friction presented the very best of South Asian music, from Bollywood to contemporary sounds.

Sandé belted out 'Lifted', accompanied by DJ, producer and writer Shahid 'Naughty Boy' Khan, and Kapoor sang Bollywood classics such as 'Mere Khwabon Mein'. Palak Muchhal and Benny Dayal represented the new wave of Bollywood.

IT DIDN'T GO PETE TONG

As well as having a name that has become part of cockney rhyming slang, veteran DJ Pete Tong is the father of the Ibiza party dance sound. To mark the 20th anniversary of Radio 1 in Ibiza in 2015, Tong presented a line-up of live artists, who performed with Jules Buckley and his Heritage Orchestra at the BBC Radio 1 Ibiza Prom, whilst Tong was perched high up at the back behind his decks.

The audience was soon on its feet, pumping fists into the air as some of the best-known party-scene songs filled the hall, from Fat Boy Slim to Moby, with vocals by Ella Eyre and John Newman.

TRIBUTE TO A STARMAN

A celebration of David Bowie's songs and music in 2016 marked his death in January of that year at the age of 69.

Artists who performed reinterpreted his work rather than just copying it, with music by the German music collective s t a r g a z e. It added up to an avant-garde feel, with a mix of Bowie's most famous songs as well as lesser-known ones. Neil Hannon of The Divine Comedy sang 'Station to Station', singer-guitarist Anna Calvi belted out 'Lady Grinning Soul', and Marc Almond had the dream double of 'Life on Mars' and 'Starman'.

The highlight was a spine-tingling version of the title track of Bowie's final album, *Black Star*, when Amanda Palmer joined Calvi on stage, with the great organ at the RAH joining in magnificently.

ALL THAT JAZZ

Jules Buckley and his Metropole Orkest celebrated jazz bass player, composer and bandleader Charles Mingus, along with featured artists for the 2017 prom Beneath the Underdog: Charles Mingus Revisited. The first half of the title was that of his autobiography.

Mingus combined the classic style of Duke Ellington and Jelly Roll Morton with the radical spirit of black music of the 1950s, 1960s and 1970s, and has influenced artists from Joni Mitchell and Elvis Costello to Debbie Harry.

American trumpet player Christian Scott opened with 'Boogie Stop Shuffle' and Kandace Springs sang 'Weird Nightmare'. Other Mingus favourites included 'Moanin'' and 'Goodbye Pork Pie Hat'. The gospel-style 'Better Git It in Your Soul' was the exhilarating finale, showcasing Leo Pellegrino on saxophone.

STILL GOT SOUL

Jools Holland and his Rhythm & Blues Orchestra paid tribute to a pioneering record label in a 2017 prom entitled Stax Records: 50 Years of Soul. The Stax Records artists who performed showed that age has done nothing to diminish soul.

Legendary musician and composer Booker T. Jones joined the likes of Tom Jones and Beverley Knight in an evening that featured hits from Otis Redding, Isaac Hayes and Johnnie Taylor. William Bell duetted with Beverley Knight on 'Private Number'. Eddie Floyd sang 'Knock on Wood' and duetted with James Morrison on Wilson Pickett's '634-5789'. Sam Moore joined Tom Jones for 'I Can't Stand Up for Falling Down' and Knight for 'Hold On, I'm Comin''.

Morrison channelled Otis Redding on 'Try a Little Tenderness' and there was a spine-tingling version of Redding's 'Dock of the Bay' sung by Jones, accompanied by Booker T. and Stax guitarist Steve Cropper.

TV FAVOURITES

Young people have been enticed to enjoy good music, including classical, at the Proms by using popular TV shows as themes ...

BLUE PETER

From 1998 to 2007 the *Blue Peter* prom was an annual fixture. This brought in hordes of young children and their families, who were entertained in various fun ways as well as getting the chance to listen to beautiful music.

In 2004, for example, the theme was 'Beating Drums, Dancing Lions', showcasing both Eastern and Western cultures. *Blue Peter* presenter Liz Barker took part in the Lion Dance, performed by a Chinese dance troupe in flamboyant lion costumes, and her fellow presenter Simon Thomas played the flute with the orchestra for Tchaikovsky's *The Nutcracker*.

With Stravinsky's *The Firebird* one moment and John Williams's 'Hedwig's Theme' from *Harry Potter* the next, the Proms aimed to show that music in all its forms can delight and entertain. A highlight was Ravel's *Bolero*, in which several members of the BBC Philharmonic made their way on stage from all over the hall, each with a different reason for being late!

At the finale, the youngsters got a taster of the Last Night by singing along to 'Land of Hope and Glory'.

The following year saw a space theme with 'Out of This World'. John Williams's stirring *Star Wars* theme built the excitement and a magician performed during Paul Dukas's *The Sorcerer's Apprentice*. Then, as the familiar *Doctor Who* theme played, a Dalek invaded the Royal Albert Hall amidst flashing lights and smoke.

JUST WHAT THE DOCTOR ORDERED

Following on from the lone Dalek invasion two years earlier, the Doctor's nemesis returned in full force in 2008 for the *Doctor Who* prom.

The Tardis was parked next to the bust of Henry Wood – who remained unperturbed. The monsters and aliens who appeared on stage and in the audience were played by the artists who had portrayed them on television. There was dramatic music from the TV series along with the likes of Gustav Holst's *The Planets*, Mark-Anthony Turnage's *Three Asteroids* and Richard Wagner's *Die Walküre* (*The Valkyrie*).

The prom was co-presented by actress Freema Agyeman, who played the Doctor's companion Martha Jones in the BBC show. Monsters from the series also appeared, including the legendary Daleks. Further reincarnations of the *Doctor Who* prom returned in the 2010 and 2013 seasons.

A SPORTING OCCASION

Gabby Logan presented a BBC Sport Prom in 2014.

The *Match of the Day* music was played, along with that of *Test Match Special*, *Wimbledon*, *Ski Sunday* and *The Horse of the Year Show*. Other sports-related themes included 'Summon the Heroes' by John Williams (the theme from the Atlanta Olympics), 'Chariots of Fire' by Vangelis and two pieces played at rugby games: Hubert Parry's 'Jerusalem' and Carl Orff's 'O Fortuna' from *Carmina Burana*. As the orchestra played, big screens in the hall showed famous sporting moments.

HOLMES, SWEET HOLMES

Not only was the world's greatest detective a mastermind of criminology, he was also an accomplished violinist who wrote a pioneering study of Dutch sacred music, tussled with a contralto from the Warsaw Opera and used Offenbach to outwit a pair of jewel thieves!

Sherlock Holmes – A Musical Mind in 2015 explored his musical passions, as well as scores from the various Holmes movies and TV series, including the recent updated version, *Sherlock*. Co-writer of this series Mark Gatiss, who also played Mycroft, joined presenter Matthew Sweet to talk about Arthur Conan Doyle's detective Holmes and his love for music. The concert included works by Paganini, Lassus and Wagner.

THAT'S LIFE!

Distinguished naturalist and broadcaster Sir David Attenborough presented a concert inspired by his acclaimed BBC TV series *Life Story* in 2015.

Attenborough introduced the musical pieces, composed by Murray Gold, and explained sequences from the series that played out on big screens as the BBC Concert Orchestra rose magnificently to the occasion. He was also joined by members of the production team, who offered insights into the making of the stunning natural history series.

STRICTLY SPEAKING

A big silver rotating glitter ball hung from the ceiling. It could only mean one thing. Yes, the *Strictly* prom of 2016.

It began with Jule Styne's *Gypsy Overture* as professional dancers Karen, Kevin and Joanne Clifton, Janette Manrara, Giovanni Pernice and Aljaž Škorjanec sashayed on and did their stuff. The evening celebrated music from Vienna to Latin America with the BBC Concert Orchestra, conducted by Gavin Sutherland.

Katie Derham, a finalist in the 2015 series of *Strictly Come Dancing*, danced the Viennese Waltz with Aljaž Skorjanec to the music of 'If I Can Dream' by Walter Earle Brown.

'I think the themed Proms are a very interesting way of bringing in a different sort of audience. In my first year as Director of the BBC Proms, we did the Strictly prom, which seemed to me to be a lovely tie-in with music and television because there is so much fantastic dance music and we were able to bring in an audience that might have, for instance, come in to see their favourite dancers from the programme, and then found themselves hearing music by Shostakovich and Richard Strauss'

– David Pickard, Director of the BBC Proms

HORRIBLY ENTERTAINING

The children's prom of 2011 was based on the CBBC TV series *Horrible Histories*, and featured a number of typically fun yet educational songs from the show along with classical music.

The performers were the six-member cast of the series, supported by the Aurora Orchestra with Nicholas Collon conducting. The Music Centre Children's Choir and Kids Company Choir served as chorus. The Horrible Histories Big Prom Party featured everything from the Savage Stone Age and the Vicious Vikings to the Gorgeous Georgians and the Vile Victorians.

KIDS' STUFF

In 2014, the BBC addressed its youngest ever audience by staging a CBeebies prom. Characters from the children's television shows, including Mr Bloom, hosted as the BBC Philharmonic played a combination of CBeebies themes and classical favourites. Music included the Hornpipe from Henry Wood's *Fantasia on British Sea-Songs* and the Dargason from Holst's *St Paul's Suite*.

'The themed Proms, such as *Strictly*, *Doctor Who* and *Blue Planet*, are really positive collaborations and bring in people who wouldn't normally buy a Proms ticket. People book because David Attenborough is there, or the *Strictly* dancers are there, and a lot of mums booked for the CBeebies prom who wouldn't normally go at all'

— Helen Heslop, BBC Live Events team manager

A ROYAL OCCASION

The Queen and HRH The Duke of Edinburgh attended a special BBC Proms concert in 2003 for the 50th anniversary of Her Majesty's coronation. It was their second visit to the Proms and the first since 1994.

The programme had a wide-ranging collection of British and Commonwealth music, including works by

Sir Michael Tippett and William Walton specially written for the Coronation year. There was also music by British composer Mark-Anthony Turnage, with his *Momentum*, and folk songs by Australian composer Percy Grainger.

Sir Andrew Davis conducted the BBC SO and five massed choirs: the BBC Symphony Chorus and BBC Singers joined the choristers of three of England's leading institutions – Winchester Cathedral, Winchester College and Eton College.

THE MANE EVENT

The Proms marked the 100th anniversary of the outbreak of the First World War in 2014 with a series of performances. The *War Horse* prom featured the life-sized horse puppets from the world-famous National Theatre production accompanied by Gareth Malone conducting the Military Wives Choir.

Music included Holst's 'Home They Brought Her Warrior Dead' and Henry Wood's 'New War Hymn'.

MOVIE MAGIC

The BBC Concert Orchestra brought to life the music of the silver screen, from Pinewood to Hollywood, from *Superman* to *Star Wars*, with a special tribute to mark the 85th birthday of one of the world's favourite movie composers, John Williams, in 2017. It also included music from *Raiders of the Lost Ark*, *E.T*, *Jaws* and the *Harry Potter* movies

In 2003 the Great British Film Music Prom cele-
brated the works of UK composers, including John
Barry. Among the works played were Barry's 'The Lion in
Winter', 'Dances with Wolves', 'From Russia with Love'
and the themes from the James Bond classics *Goldfinger* and
From Russia With Love.

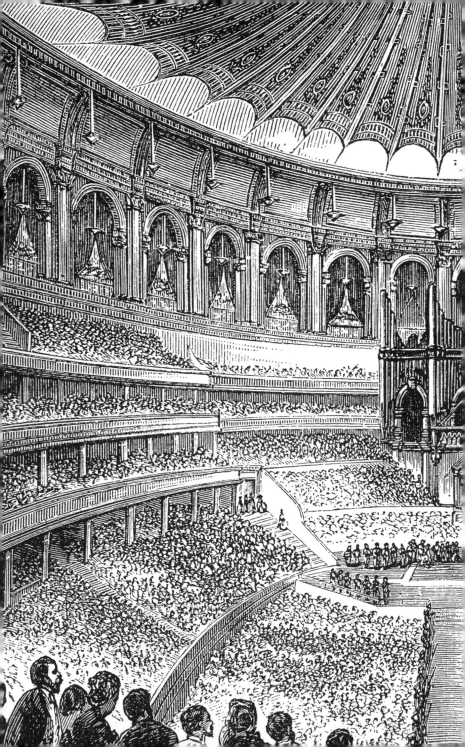